Index

G000111916

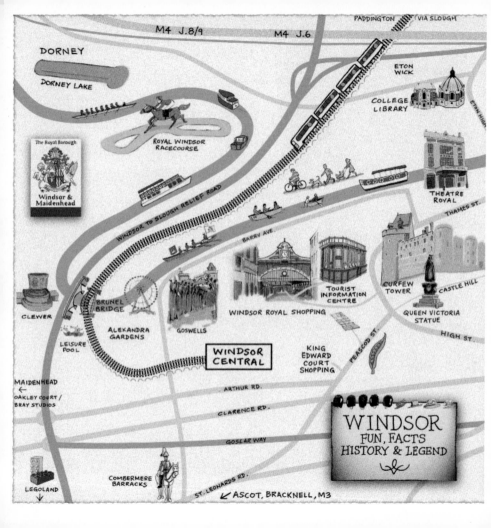

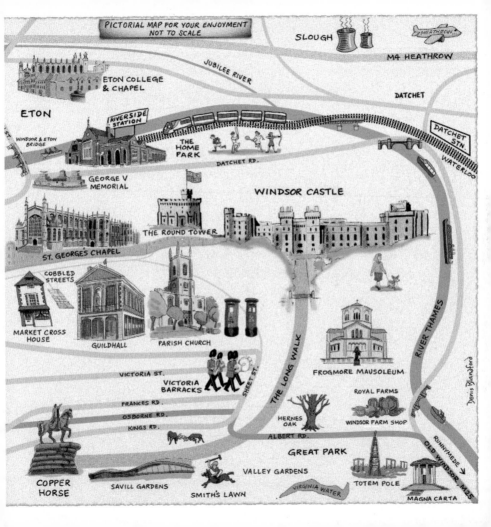

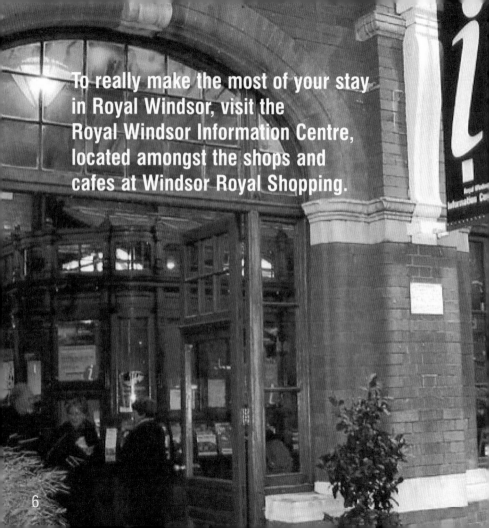

To really make the most of your stay in Royal Windsor, visit the Royal Windsor Information Centre, located amongst the shops and cafes at Windsor Royal Shopping.

The Royal Windsor Information Centre is open 7 days a week, the staff are friendly and knowledgeable and can help with a range of services for visitors and local residents including:

- Accommodation Booking Service

- Tickets for attractions and events such as Legoland, Boat Trips, Bus Tours, Guided Walking Tours, Racing at Ascot and Windsor, The Royal Windsor Horse Show, Royal Windsor Tattoo and Windsor Festival.

- Local information including: What's On, train and bus timetables, guide books and postcards.

The Royal Borough

Windsor & Maidenhead

Contact us on
+44 (0)1753 743900
email: windsor.tic@rbwm.gov.uk

24-hour information visit
www.windsor.gov.uk

Windsor

In prehistoric times, enormous glaciers stood within 20 miles of Windsor and the huge quantities of water from the melting ice carved the route of the River Thames.

The River found its natural path through thick forests and the remains of mammoth and rhinoceros have been found here.

The original 7th century Saxon settlement of Windlesora was located a mile or so down the road in Old Windsor.

After the creation of the Castle, a new settlement sprang up around its walls which was known as New Windsor to distinguish it from Old Windsor.

Windsor was called New Windsor until 1974 when Windsor merged into one borough with Maidenhead.

The name Windsor comes from the Anglo Saxon winch-on-a-riverbank. A winch would have been used to pull the boats up and over the shallows of the Thames or to unload boats bringing supplies for the castle and town.

Windlesora is also understood to mean winding shore.

Windsor Castle

The original Castle was built on a 30 metre (100 feet) chalk cliff rising above the river. The nearby settlement of Clewer means cliff-dwellers.

Windsor Castle is the oldest and largest inhabited Castle in the world. People have lived here continuously since it was built nearly 1000 years ago.

King Henry I was the first monarch to use Windsor Castle as a royal residence.

In 1666 Samuel Pepys proclaimed the Castle the most romantique castle that is in the world. That is still true today. Romantic was spelt like that in those days!

Her Majesty The Queen makes her home at Windsor most weekends, at Easter and the week of Royal Ascot - Buckingham Palace is her office!

Windsor attracts over 1 million visitors per year with 35% of those from overseas. Just over half of them have visited before.

55% of the international visitors are from non-English speaking countries.

Over 300 people work in the Castle helping run the Royal residence, 150 of those live inside the Castle walls.

Building the Castle

Windsor Castle was built by William the Conqueror, following his invasion of England in 1066.

The Doomsday book clearly states that the Crown rented the land the Castle is built on, for twelve shillings a year for five hundred years from the Lords of the Clewer Manor estate.

The Castle walls are 4 metres (16 feet) thick in places.

The Castle was built on the steep cliff overlooking the River Thames holding a strategic position and is part of a ring of castles around London. The Tower of London is the centre of the ring and was only one day's march from Windsor.

The original Castle structure was built from wood with earth fortifications. The Castle was later rebuilt in stone once the earth had settled.

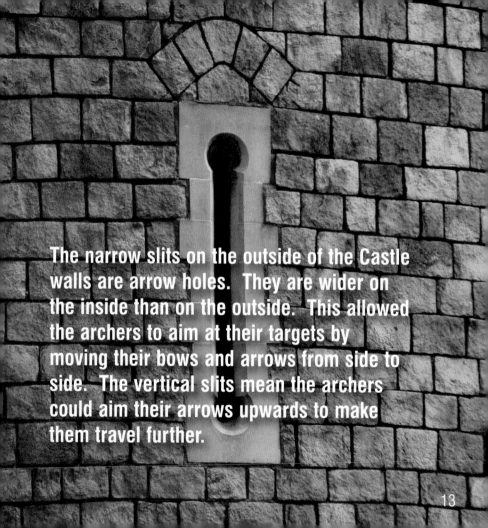

The narrow slits on the outside of the Castle walls are arrow holes. They are wider on the inside than on the outside. This allowed the archers to aim at their targets by moving their bows and arrows from side to side. The vertical slits mean the archers could aim their arrows upwards to make them travel further.

13

For centuries the river was the only way to transport goods between towns due to the lack of decent roads. Stone and wood were imported by barge to the waterfront of Windsor and used in the building of the Castle, St George's Chapel and Eton College.

Windsor Castle covers approximately 13 acres (5.26 hectares) and is almost one mile in circumference.

Windsor Castle is spread over the equivalent of 269 tennis courts and is more like a fortified town.

Boiling fat, water and possibly tar could be poured over enemies trying to get into the Castle through King Henry VIII's gate from the 'murder holes' in the ceiling of the gate. There are also good examples of murder holes in the Norman Gate.

There are rumours of a maze of tunnels having been built from the Castle to buildings throughout the town and they would have been extremely useful if they had existed in large numbers. However despite several subterranean vaults being discovered under the High Street, there is only one tunnel that runs in the opposite direction to the town and a sally port, long since blocked up that leaves the base of the Curfew Tower. A sally port was a wide tunnel built to allow many troops to leave a Castle if it was being besieged and to surprise the attacking troops from behind.

The second emblem from the left of the gate is a Pomegranate which was King Henry VIII's first wife, Catherine of Aragon's symbol. A pomegranate represents faithfulness - something that Henry VIII definitely did not have as he divorced Catherine and went on to marry another 5 wives!

It is thought that the extensive remodelling of Windsor Castle by King Edward III between 1344 and 1348 was financed mostly from ransoms paid by the prisoners kept in the Castle, who had moaned continuously about their poor living conditions.

The Round Tower

The Round Tower is 800 years old and was built on an artificial mound. It has a dry moat which now contains beautiful gardens which are occasionally open to the public.

The Round Tower is built over a well which drops 165 feet into rock. The well would provide essential water for the troops when the Castle was under siege. The Castle was under siege in 1193 and again in 1216. There was also a short lived siege in 1262.

The Round Tower is 65.5m (215 feet) above the level of the River Thames and 85.3m (280 feet) above sea level.

In the early 19th century George IV added an extra 10m (33 feet) to the Round Tower to make it look more imposing.

The grass on the mound of the Round Tower is notoriously difficult to cut. The gardeners attach an electric lawn mower to a strong rope which they lower down the mound and then pull back up the bank.

The Round Tower is not round.
The tower follows the mound it
was built on and is actually oval!

Banquets

The Queen is Head of State of the United Kingdom of Great Britain and Northern Ireland. As such, she often welcomes foreign Heads of State at Windsor when they visit the country and entertains her guests to banquets in St George's Hall.

Windsor is decorated with flags and banners for such occasions and The Queen will accompany the visiting Head of State in a ceremonial procession through the town.

State occasions are funded from the Civil List and sometimes by the Foreign Office as they are a major benefit to relations between the two countries. Up to 6 months planning goes into a each single state visit.

Banquet guests sit at a 160-year-old-dining table made of Cuban mahogany which is 53m (175 feet) in length and is assembled using 68 40cm (15 inch) sections. At the table's maximum, it can seat 160 people.

The Civil List is funded by the profits from the Crown Estate.

State Banquets were not always held at Windsor. It was Prince Philip's idea to move some of them when possible from Buckingham Palace. This break in Royal tradition caused some logistical headaches but has been very popular amongst hosts and visitors. Some State Banquets still take place at Buckingham Palace in London.

A footman stands on the table and moves around dusters with his feet to polish the table. He also positions the flower arrangements and candelabra whilst on the table. Just before the guests arrive for dinner he returns to the table to light the candles. The term footman didn't come from polishing tables though!

No table cloths are used because of the highly polished finish on the table.

The term footman means simply man on foot as opposed to 'man on horse' as those low down in the household 'pecking' order never went anywhere on a horse. Footmen often used to run alongside moving carriages too!

It takes 8-10 people 2 days to lay the table and a stick is used to measure the distance from each chair back to the edge of the banquet table. Each guest is allocated 46cm (18 inches).

The Queen approves all banquet menus and makes her own suggestions on occasion. The Queen also personally inspects the hall, table and decorations on the afternoon before a banquet.

The Queen has a choice of 47 porcelain desert services to use. They include Royal Doulton, Sévres, Limoges and Royal Copenhagen services.

Each place setting has 6 glasses: white wine, red wine, port, water plus two champagne glasses. One for pudding and one for the after dinner toast.

The pats of butter are rolled into a ball and then hand stamped with a crown. As a child The Queen used to help with this task.

The Queen's dinner service has 4,000 items including 288 dinner plates.

For each banquet, the Castle catering team chooses from one of six favourite napkin folds - there is even one called Prince of Wales feathers.

Precise timing is crucial when serving so many guests at the same time, so butlers and footmen are prompted to begin serving by a blue and amber traffic light system discretely installed at the end of the hall.

All the dishes of food are scrutinized by a chef before being served at a banquet.

"I can only assume that it is largely due to the accumulation of toasts to my health over the years that I am still enjoying a fairly satisfactory state of health and have reached such an unexpectedly great age", said The Duke of Edinburgh on reaching his 80th birthday.

By dawn, every plate, glass or item of cutlery has been washed up, dried and in some cases polished and put away.

The Queen likes her meat well done and the royal chef always identifies her portions of food with a sprig of parsley or unique decoration so the footman knows which piece to serve her!

At Royal Banquets, The Queen likes to put her own seasoning on her food.

Lamb, milk and vegetables come from the Home Park in Windsor with salmon and beef from Balmoral in Scotland and game and crabs from Sandringham in Norfolk.

Every royal chef has to be briefed on what 'not' to serve to The Queen. The no-go list includes garlic, onions, tomato sauce, shellfish, curry and messy foods such as spaghetti.

Chicken, game and fish are always boned for The Queen and her guests.

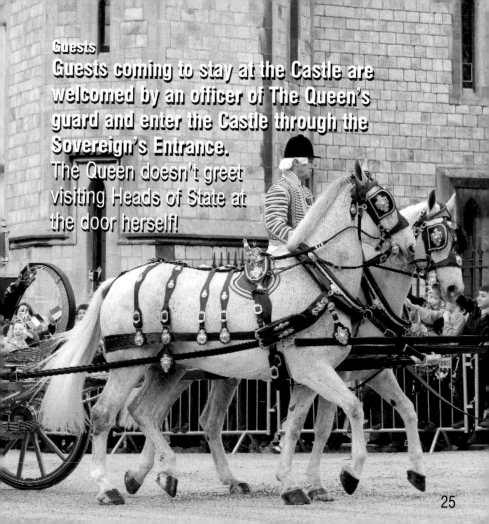

Guests

Guests coming to stay at the Castle are welcomed by an officer of The Queen's guard and enter the Castle through the Sovereign's Entrance.

The Queen doesn't greet visiting Heads of State at the door herself!

Housekeeping staff will unpack a guest's cases making a note of each item of clothing, jewellery and personal items. Plastic coat hangers are replaced! Gowns are hung and jewellery laid out. When the guest leaves, the staff repack everything in the same order and wrap clothes with tissue paper – sometimes this can take between 3 to 4 hours.

The Royal Librarian prepares a display of appropriate pictures and artefacts from the 300,000 books, drawings and prints housed at the Castle.

State guest rooms overlook the Long Walk and have his & hers bathrooms.

Waterloo Chamber
The Waterloo Chamber was renamed The Music Room for an evening in June 2004 when, during a visit by the French President Jacques Chirac, the musical 'Les Miserables' was performed! The Waterloo Chamber was so named to commemorate Wellington's 1815 defeat of Napoleon.

Some of the large pictures are not actually in the frames. The frames are attached to the walls and the picture hung in between.

19 State visits have been hosted at Windsor including:

1972	Queen Juliana and Prince Bernhard of The Netherlands
1978	President and Senhora Eanes of Portugal
1982	President and Mrs Reagan of the United States
1991	President and Mrs Walesa of Poland
2000	Queen Margrethe II and Prince Hendrik of Denmark
2001	President and Mrs Mbeki of South Africa
2001	King Abdullah II and Queen Rania of Jordan
2004	President and Madame Chirac of France (To mark the centenary of the Entente Cordiale in 2004)
2008	President and Madame Sarkozy of France
2009	Her Excellency Smt Pratibha Devisingh Patil, President of India
2008	In June outgoing US President George W Bush popped in for tea with The Queen during his farewell tour. He arrived in his official helicopter Marine One and literally stayed an hour!

Flags

A Union Flag (Union Jack) flies at Windsor Castle all the time as the Castle is technically classed as a fortress. When The Queen is in residence the Castle goes from being a fortress to that of a Royal Palace and, as such, the Union Flag is taken down and replaced by the Royal Standard.

About 20 minutes before The Queen is expected at the Castle the flag man will climb the steps to the Round Tower. As this takes quite a while, a phone is installed at the top just in case The Queen is delayed. The flag man will watch the final minutes of The Queen's progress towards the Castle through his binoculars. He hoists the Royal Standard on the flag pole in the Round Tower as soon as Queen is inside the Castle grounds. The Queen is then officially In Residence.

There is an assigned flag man at both Windsor Castle and Buckingham Palace whose specific responsibility is to take care of the flags. A flag man will, of course, have other duties when not attending to the flags.

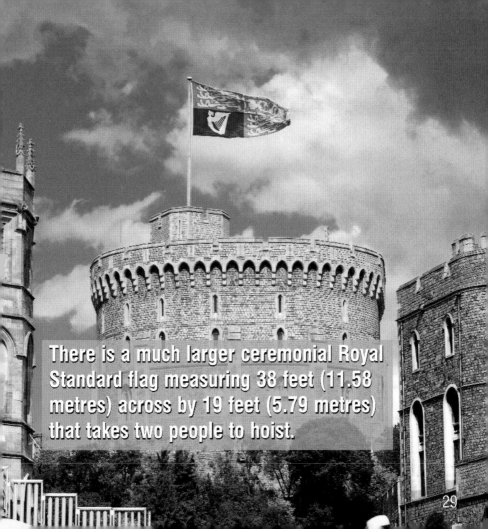

There is a much larger ceremonial Royal Standard flag measuring 38 feet (11.58 metres) across by 19 feet (5.79 metres) that takes two people to hoist.

This larger ceremonial Royal Standard is flown at Windsor Castle on very special occasions such as The Queen's Official Birthday (2nd Saturday in June), her real birthday (21st April), Garter Service day and was also raised to mark the wedding of HRH Prince Charles to Camilla, the Duchess of Cornwall. Occasionally even during these special occasions the smaller Royal Standard replaces the ceremonial Royal Standard if there are very high winds!

A miniature Royal Standard is flown on The Queen's car while undertaking official journeys and even on aeroplanes before and after take off.

Formerly, on older aeroplanes, VC10 for example, the hole in the cockpit roof (used for navigator's sextant) had the flag poked out of it! These days they have to use the sliding left hand side window.

The Royal Standard is flown at Ascot Racecourse, the pavilion at Smiths Lawn and at the Royal Windsor Horse Show whenever the Queen visits.

Clocks

The Windsor Castle estate including Windsor Great Park has over 450 clocks ranging from beautiful miniature chiming gold timepieces to a clock tower overlooking the cricket pavilion. When British Summer Time (BST) begins, it takes The Queen's clock maker 16 hours to move every clock forward by one hour. At the end of BST it takes him 18 hours to adjust every clock back one hour (as he actually has to move them forward 11 hours!! Confusing eh?).

Fireplaces

The many fireplaces in Windsor Castle are maintained by two fender smiths. It is their responsibility to make sure that fires are prepared and lit before guests enter a room.

Great Fire of Windsor
Fire broke out on The Queen and Duke of Edinburgh's 45th Wedding Anniversary.

The 1992 fire started when a workman's electric lamp ignited a curtain whilst the Castle was being renovated to install a new wiring system. The old wiring was deemed unsafe and a dangerous fire risk!

The fire took 250 fire fighters 16 hours to put out and 1.5 million litres of water. Some of the water used to put out the fire was from the River Thames via the pumping house by Romney Lock.

The fire destroyed 20% of the Castle's State Apartments and renovations took 5 years at a cost of £37 million.

Days after the fire the Castle was reopened so people could see the damage.

The Duke of Edinburgh commissioned a special replacement stained glass window for the private chapel. The window commemorates the fire and shows firefighters extinquishing the blaze.

St George's Chapel

Building

The Chapel is dedicated to St George, St Edward the Confessor and the Virgin Mary but is commonly referred to as St George's Chapel. St George is the Patron Saint of England.

There are at least three services held in the Chapel every day of the year and the public are welcome to attend.

St George's Chapel is a Royal Peculiar. The chapel is not subject to the jurisdiction of any Bishop or Archbishop but the Dean and Canons of Windsor (the priests who run St George's) who are appointed by The Queen. There are only two Royal Peculiars in the country, the other is Westminster Abbey. As a consequence, The Dean and Canons own one quarter of Windsor Castle freehold, that is the Chapel and all the surrounding buildings.

St George's is entirely self funding and receives no money from church or state. The inside of the Chapel is simply breathtaking.

A buttress is a supporting wall built at a right angle against an outside wall and St George's Chapel has flying buttresses. See how the supports extend at an angle and join the building further up.

There is a series of animals on top of the buttresses known as the King's Beasts.

The Beasts are unicorns, falcons, harts, bulls, swans, lions, dragons, panthers, greyhounds and antelopes, and are associated with the Lancastrian and York Royal families. Some of the beasts are holding flagpoles – but these flagpoles are in fact lightning conductors.

The original 15th century beasts were in a dangerous state by the 17th century and were removed in about 1672. The current beasts were put in place in the 1920s.

More recent stone carving has been provided by the students of the City & Guilds in London to replace some of the decayed grotesques below the windows on the outside of the Chapel. Grotesques are the distorted carved stone animals and beasts that adorn the outside of the Chapel.

Royal Weddings have usually taken place in public but in a break with tradition, The Queen's fourth child and third son HRH Prince Edward married Sophie Rhys-Jones in St George's Chapel on 19th June 1999. After the ceremony they rode through the town in an open-topped carriage. Edward and Sophie became the Earl and Countess of Wessex upon their marriage.

The Princess Royal's son, Peter Phillips married American, Autumn Kelly at St George's Chapel on 17th May 2008.

Tombs and Vaults

The Chapel contains the mortal remains of 10 Kings of England. The earliest are those of Henry VI and Edward IV. Also within the Chapel is the sword of Edward III – the sword first hung in an earlier Chapel in the Castle so predates today's Chapel by about 120 years.

Henry VIII and his favourite third Queen, Jane Seymour, are buried here. Jane predeceased Henry by 10 years and was the love of Henry's life. However they are not alone, even in death!

After his beheading at Whitehall in London, the remains of King Charles I were placed in the same vault as Henry and Jane. His head was sewn back onto his body on the kitchen table of The Deanery, adjoining the Chapel.

Her Majesty, Queen Elizabeth The Queen Mother, who died at the age of 101 in 2002, is buried in St George's Chapel with her husband King George VI. The ashes of her daughter Princess Margaret who predeceased her by 7 weeks were interred in the same vault.

Order of The Garter

Becoming a Garter Knight has been the personal gift of the Monarch since 23rd April 1348 when Edward III instituted his son (the Black Prince) and 24 of his most trusted supporters as Knights of the Garter. Today the Order still consists of 24 English Knights.

Some say that King Edward III's new chivalric order was named after his supposed lover, the Countess of Salisbury, dropped her garter at a ball in Windsor.

It is more likely to be called 'Garter' after the straps that keep armour in place - symbolically holding the Monarch and his 24 knights together as one.

Nowadays the Garter Service takes place at Windsor Castle in early June on the Monday of Royal Ascot week.

During the procession to St George's Chapel, Knights of the Garter wear long deep blue velvet robes, white plumed feather caps and blue garters. The Queen hosts a lunch at the Castle before the service.

On St George's Day (23 April 2008) The Queen made Prince William the 1000th Knight of the Garter.

Each Knight has his coat of Arms placed on St George's Hall ceiling. Additionally in St George's Chapel a banner hangs above his or her seat together with a crest, helmet and sword. Lady Garter Knights don't have a sword!

Military Knights of Windsor

The Military Knights of Windsor were established by Edward III and their official role is to pray for the Monarch and Knights of the Garter.

There are up to 12 Military Knights all of whom live inside the Castle walls in the houses opposite the Chapel. They are all retired army officers, some in their 80s or older.

Only the Governor of the Military Knights, who lives in the Mary Tudor Tower in the middle of the houses opposite the Chapel, has actually been knighted by The Queen and is a real 'Sir'.

Choristers

St George's School opposite the Windsor & Eton Riverside Station is where the choristers for St George's Chapel go to school. The choristers are 24 boys aged between 7 and 13 who sing services in the Chapel six days a week in term time. The school has 400 boys and girls all together.

The school is connected to the Castle by 104 steps. The steps are known as the 100 Steps.

The Guard Mounting ceremony known as The Changing of the Guard, takes place at 11am every day (except Sundays) between April and July and alternate days throughout the rest of the year.

Soldiers

Windsor Castle Guards and Duties
The new guard accompanied by pipes and drums marches up through the town to the Castle from the Victoria Barracks. If you are planning a visit and specifically want to see the Changing of the Guard, please check details beforehand.

There is always a full band when The Queen is in residence.

The Guards' duty is to protect the Monarch and their duties are split into two hour shifts. When on duty the Guards stand in position by sentry boxes (in case of rain) and from time to time they will march up and down in a defined area by their guarding post. In the case of an emergency any of the Guards are poised ready for action in a heartbeat.

It is OK to have your photo taken beside a Guard but it is not OK to make them laugh or distract them in anyway.

The Guard consists of one Officer, five NCOs (non commissioned officers), one Drummer and 21 Guardsmen. Some sentries are doubled when The Queen is in residence.

The Guards, in their spectacular uniforms, are still modern soldiers whose operational duties take them around the world to areas of conflict such as Afghanistan, the Gulf and Bosnia.

Soldiers from a Battalion of Foot Guards are stationed at Victoria Barracks. Windsor has two barracks in the town, the other being Combermere Barracks which is used by the Household Cavalry.

Visiting regiments such as The Gurkhas, Royal Marines and RAF have also mounted the Windsor Castle Guard since the Second World War.

When the Court is in residence, the guard mounting is held in the Quadrangle inside the Castle and in the winter, it takes place just inside the Castle on the parade ground near Henry VIII's Gate.

Uniforms, Plumes and Bearskins

The uniforms of the Foot Guards look identical from a distance, but are very different.

Each guard has a scarlet tunic with dark blue collar, shoulder epaulettes piped in white, cuffs of dark blue and a white leather belt. Their trousers are dark blue with a red stripe down the side. However the uniform of each regiment differs slightly in the colour of the plume in the bearskin cap, the distancing of the buttons on the front and cuffs of the tunics and insignia on the collars. Some officers wear a gold or crimson sash.

Since 1815 the Guards, topped their ceremonial uniforms with bearskin caps in memory of the victory over the French at the Battle of Waterloo.

In 1815 there were only Grenadier, Coldstream and Scots Guards. The Irish Guards were formed in 1900 and the Welsh Guards during World War I.

A soldier's bearskin is 18 inches tall, weighs 1.5 pounds and is made from the thick fur of the Canadian Brown Bear, which has been dyed black. The British Army purchases the hats, which are known as caps, from a British hat maker, who sources the pelts at international auctions. The hat makers purchase between 50 and 100 bear skins each year at a cost of about £650 each. Some bearskin caps in use today are more than 100 years old.

Plumes are made of horse hair and are situated on the bearskins so that the guards can easily identify each other and generals can see the regiments from a distance.

Who's Who of Guardsmen

Grenadier Guards - white plume on left side and buttons in 1s
Coldstream Guards - red plume on right side and buttons in 2s
Scots Guards - no plume and buttons in 3s
Irish Guards - blue plume on right side and buttons in 4s
Welsh Guards - green and white plume on left side and buttons in 5s

GRENADIER   COLDSTREAM   SCOTS   IRISH   WELSH

A bearskin is sometimes referred to as a busby which is incorrect. Bearskins are much taller than the hussar busby and rifle busby.

The Household Regiment
The Household Cavalry Regiment was formed on 1st October 1992 in Windsor.

It is the union of two squadrons of Life Guards (scarlet tunics and long white plumes on brass helmets) and two squadrons of Blues & Royals (navy tunics and long scarlet plumes on brass helmets) and the Royal Dragoon Guards. The mounted parts of the Household Cavalry are based in London and Windsor. When in London they are at Knightsbridge and can be seen in Whitehall carrying out the duties of The Queen's Life Guard. At Windsor they use Combermere Barracks just outside the town centre.

The Household Division is made up of seven Regiments, The Household Cavalry Regiment (The Life Guards and The Blues and Royals) and the Foot Guards Regiment (Grenadier, Coldstream, Scots, Irish and Welsh).

49

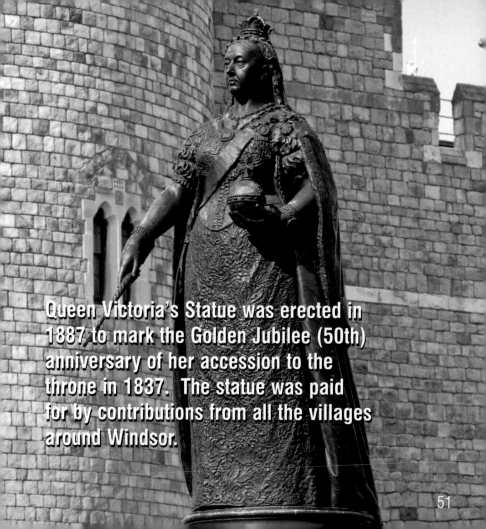

Queen Victoria's Statue was erected in 1887 to mark the Golden Jubilee (50th) anniversary of her accession to the throne in 1837. The statue was paid for by contributions from all the villages around Windsor.

51

Surrounding the Castle

Queen Victoria's Statue
The statue is made of metal which is unusual as the sculptor, Austrian Sir Joseph Edgar Boehm worked in marble most of the time. There is a memorial to Sir Joseph in St George's Chapel.

Important proclamations are made from the statue and in 1952 Elizabeth II was proclaimed Queen on the death of her father King George VI.

Peascod Street (straight ahead in front of Queen Victoria's Statue)
Pronounced Pes'cod Street by the locals.

Peascod Street leads directly down the hill from Queen Victoria's statue just outside the Castle and led to the pea fields. The name is thought to derive from pea pods. Peas and beans were an important part of the medieval diet.

Goswell Hill, or Breakneck Alley as it was known, turns off to the right from near the top of Peascod Street to the side of Central Station. This area of Windsor was the slum area of the town in 1800s. Horses often broke their necks travelling up and down the road and the alternate raised cobbles were laid to give horses more grip.

The iconic music club of the 60s, The Ricky-Tick Club (1962 – 1967), was started in the Star & Garter Hotel in Peascod Street and then moved to Barry Avenue next to the swimming pool (now the Windsor Leisure Centre).

The bands that played at the Tick were in their infancy - some later becoming rock legends in their own right. Tick bands included: Pink Floyd, The Rolling Stones, Eric Clapton, Elton John, The Who, Georgie Fame & The Blue Flames,

The Animals, The Yardbirds, Moody Blues, Van Morrison, Fleetwood Mac, Rod Stewart, Jeff Beck and Long John Baldry.

Amongst the visiting Americans were Stevie Wonder, Bill Haley & The Comets, Muddy Waters, Ben E King, Solomon Burke, Tina Turner, Bo Didley and the then unknown Jimmy Hendrix.

Star & Garter was famous as being the oldest coaching inn in Windsor and also the one-time home to the boxing fraternity where famous boxers like Sugar Ray Robinson trained above the one-time stables. The archway to the stables can still be seen today.

The creeping space fungus in the ground breaking TV drama 'The Quatermass Experiment' oozed over the viaduct walls in Goswell Hill, Windsor.

Stations in Windsor

By 1851 Windsor had two branch lines and two railway stations, the Windsor & Eton Riverside and Windsor Central Station. Windsor still has two railway stations.

The Crown and Eton College both objected to the building of the railway line connecting Windsor to London. Dr Hawtrey, the headmaster of Eton College, protested that the boys would use the railway to travel up to London for 'vice' and would throw stones at the trains. The Crown was unhappy about many aspects - even the effect of the smoke on its newly refurbished walls!

There was a specially constructed Royal Waiting Room at Windsor and Eton Riverside Station which can still be seen today adjoining the main station building. There is another Royal Waiting Room at the Central Station which is now the bar alongside the full-size replica Royal Steam Engine.

The Windsor Tourist Information Office is situated in the Central Station concourse in the old ticket hall.

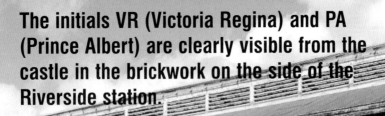

The initials VR (Victoria Regina) and PA (Prince Albert) are clearly visible from the castle in the brickwork on the side of the Riverside station.

The 7 tall blue archways with 14 doors at the side of the station were designed to enable the Household Cavalry to enter the station and board the special military trains without dismounting.

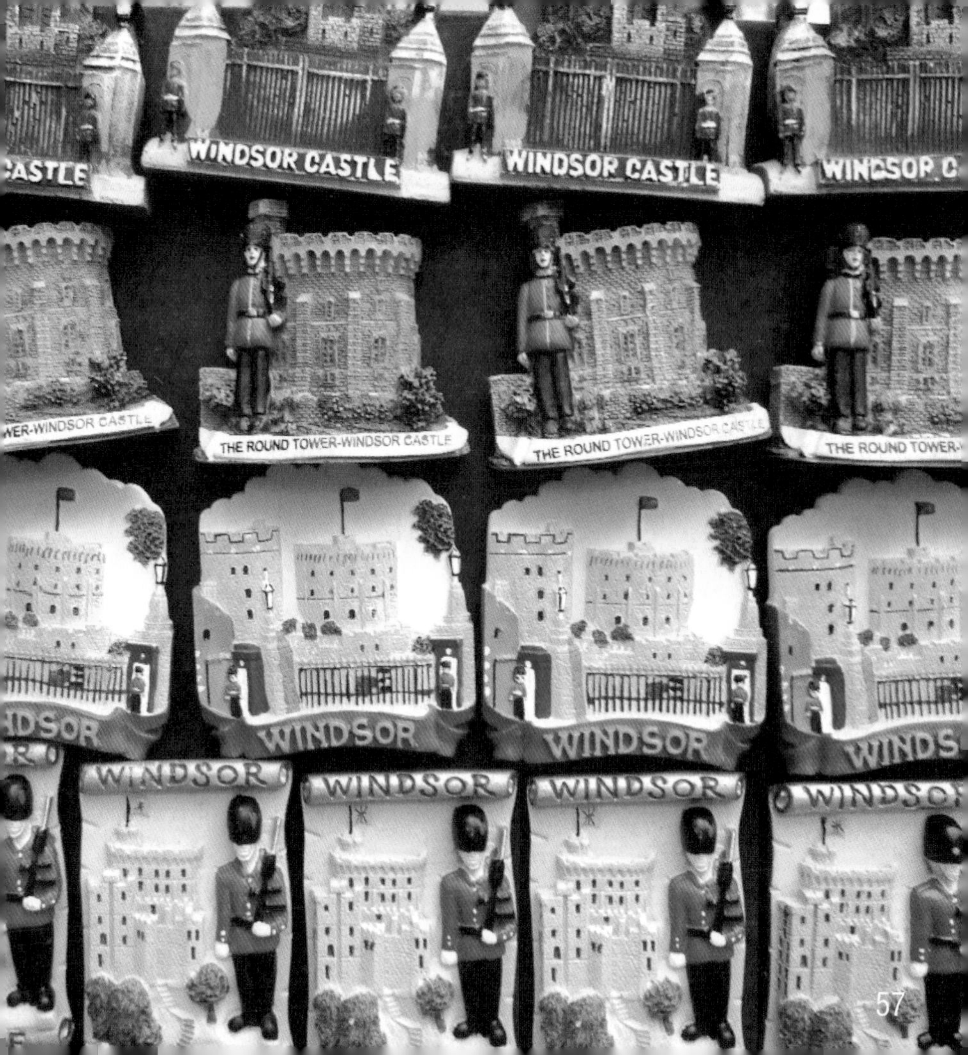

Windsor Royal Shopping is located in the stunning grade II listed Victorian Railway Station, built in 1851. It is a 'must-visit' shopping experience.

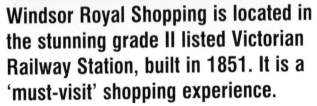

The Centre beautifully blends an eclectic mix of 40 shops and eateries with original station features including a replica Royal Steam train, cobble stones, ticket office and station concourse. There is even a Royal Waiting Room in one of the bars!

From high end fashion boutiques, jewellers and specialist perfumeries, shopping heaven is paces away from the Castle and available 7 days a week.

With 12 Cafés and Restaurants located throughout the Centre, many with terrace seating, you can sit and watch the world go by whilst enjoying a drink or bite to eat.

Stop by and be one of the Windsor Royal Shopping's 160,000 – 180,000 weekly visitors.

For the latest news and events please visit www.windsorroyalshopping.co.uk

Windsor *Royal* Shopping
a unique shopping and eating experience

Thames Street (right of Victoria's Statue as you leave the Castle)

Curfew Tower

Curfew Tower, built in 1229 was the original defensive tower for the Castle. The Tower is now a bell tower where 8 bells are rung on Royal Birthdays, Christian festivals, weddings and tolled at funerals.

The last person to be executed by hanging from the Curfew Tower was a butcher named Mark Fytton in 1536. He was executed after being caught selling poached deer meat from Windsor Great Park. However there is another story that he was executed for his religious views because of the example of Tudor graffiti chiselled into the stonework at the bottom of the Curfew Tower.

THIS ISN'T JUST DEER MEAT..... ... IT'S WINDSOR GREAT PARK DEER MEAT!

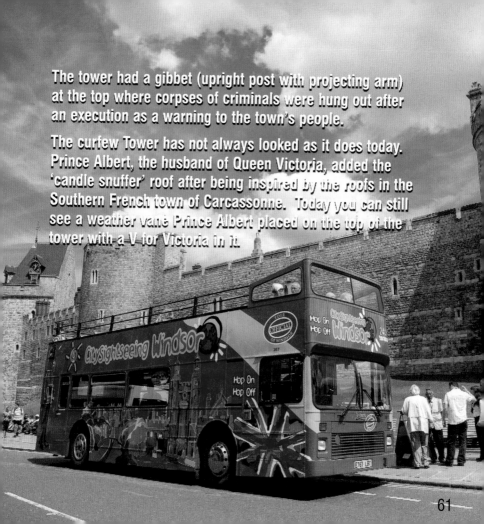

The tower had a gibbet (upright post with projecting arm) at the top where corpses of criminals were hung out after an execution as a warning to the town's people.

The curfew Tower has not always looked as it does today. Prince Albert, the husband of Queen Victoria, added the 'candle snuffer' roof after being inspired by the roofs in the Southern French town of Carcassonne. Today you can still see a weather vane Prince Albert placed on the top of the tower with a V for Victoria in it.

Those sentenced to be hanged could take up to 20 minutes to die. However, if you were 'lucky' to have friends or relatives in the crowd of spectators, they could come and pull on your ankles to help the noose tighten round your neck so you would die more quickly. This is where the term 'hangers on' came from.

Before the war Hitler took a liking to Windsor Castle and decided that he would make it one of his homes once he had conquered England. Consequently, the Castle was not bombed during the war. A rumour that British intelligence got wind of Hitler's plan and moved the Crown Jewels to the cellars here for their safety is untrue.

The tower is called the Curfew Tower because at the time it was finished there was a lights out curfew of 8pm in the town.

The iron rods sunk in the kerb on the inside bend of Castle Hill under the Curfew Tower date from the 1800s. They were used as braking wedges for the wheels of horse-drawn carriages to rest on so they wouldn't roll back down the hill. Today's taxi rank occupies the same position.

Curfew Yard

You could easily miss the passage way leading to Curfew Yard which is on the opposite side of the road from the Curfew Tower. The yard was redeveloped in the 1960s but you can still walk round the medieval building in the centre of the yard. There is evidence in the basement of the shop of a sally port (wide tunnel) coming from the castle, mentioned earlier.

Pavement Clock

In the 1950s a clock half a metre (approximately 15 inches) in diameter was installed in the pavement outside Dyson's jewellers shop at 9 Thames Street. The clock became one of the must-see sights of Windsor and remained in the pavement long after the shop closed. All that remains today is the mysterious brass outline of the clock.

Boots Passage

King Edward VII's Gateway is in Thames Street right opposite the Curfew Tower. It is known locally as Boots Passage.

The passageway was created by Jesse Boot and is an early example of 'you are here' advertising. Mr Boot was the proprietor of the Boots chain of chemists and in 1917 commissioned McDonald Gill to create a blue and white tiled replica map of Windsor Castle as it was in 1667.

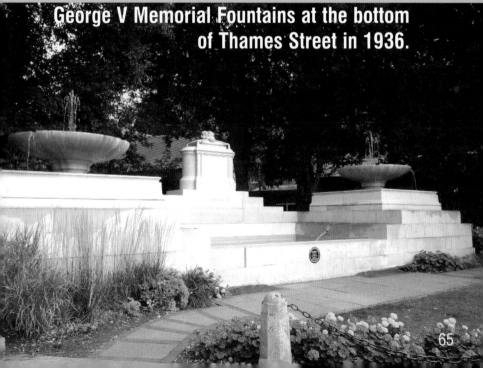

George V Memorial
Sir Edwin Lutyens often referred to as 'the greatest British architect' designed the King George V Memorial Fountains at the bottom of Thames Street in 1936.

Theatre Royal
A theatre was originally built in the High Street in 1793 and George III attended regularly when in residence at the castle. One side of the lower tier of boxes was reserved for him and his entourage and The King and Queen were provided with throne-like armchairs and programmes printed on silk.

George V Memorial
However, various disasters struck the theatre building and finances over the years until a fire destroyed it in February 1908 and Windsor was without a theatre. Fortunately the theatre's then owner, Sir William Shipley, was a prosperous and public spirited man who was determined that the old building should be replaced by one worthy of its setting. The present building was completed in 1910 and opened on 17th December that year.

The Queen and almost every other member of the Royal Family have seen performances here.

Today the theatre hosts independent plays typically running for three weeks to an average audience of 14,000. Many plays are destined for London's West End.

THEATRE ROYAL

BEYOND REASONABLE DOUBT

The Theatre car-park
Slums had to be cleared for Windsor's first car-park in River Street. The red brick building at the entrance housed public baths and the toilets. You can still spend a penny there today!

Royal Windsor Horse Show

The show was founded in 1943 and was originally conceived as a one-day event for horses and dogs to raise money for the war effort and was attended by King George VI. Dogs were banned after the first year - according to legend after a badly behaved lurcher stole a chicken drumstick from King George VI's plate.

The Royal Windsor Horse Show still has strong royal connections and The Queen often enters her own horses in the event. The Queen, the Duke of Edinburgh, Princess Anne and her daughter Zara Phillips have all competed in the past.

The show takes place in May and is the biggest outdoor horse show in the country spread over five-days with 3,000 competing horses and 70,000 people attending - all taking place in the Queen's back garden.

The Queen, the Duke of Edinburgh and other members of the Royal Family attend each day of the show.

Royal Windsor Tattoo

The Windsor Castle Royal Tattoo takes place on the evenings of the Royal Windsor Horse Show and is a celebration of the capabilities of today's forces (Royal Navy, Army and Royal Air Force). The programme consists of International and British military acts, massed bands, pipes and drums, modern military re-enactments with a fantastic finale.

This show is interspersed with ceremonial acts including the Household Cavalry's Musical Ride (which they have performed since 1882) and the Musical Drive of the King's Troop Royal Horse Artillery.

The Tattoo is a not-for-profit event, with all money raised going to the Royal British Legion.

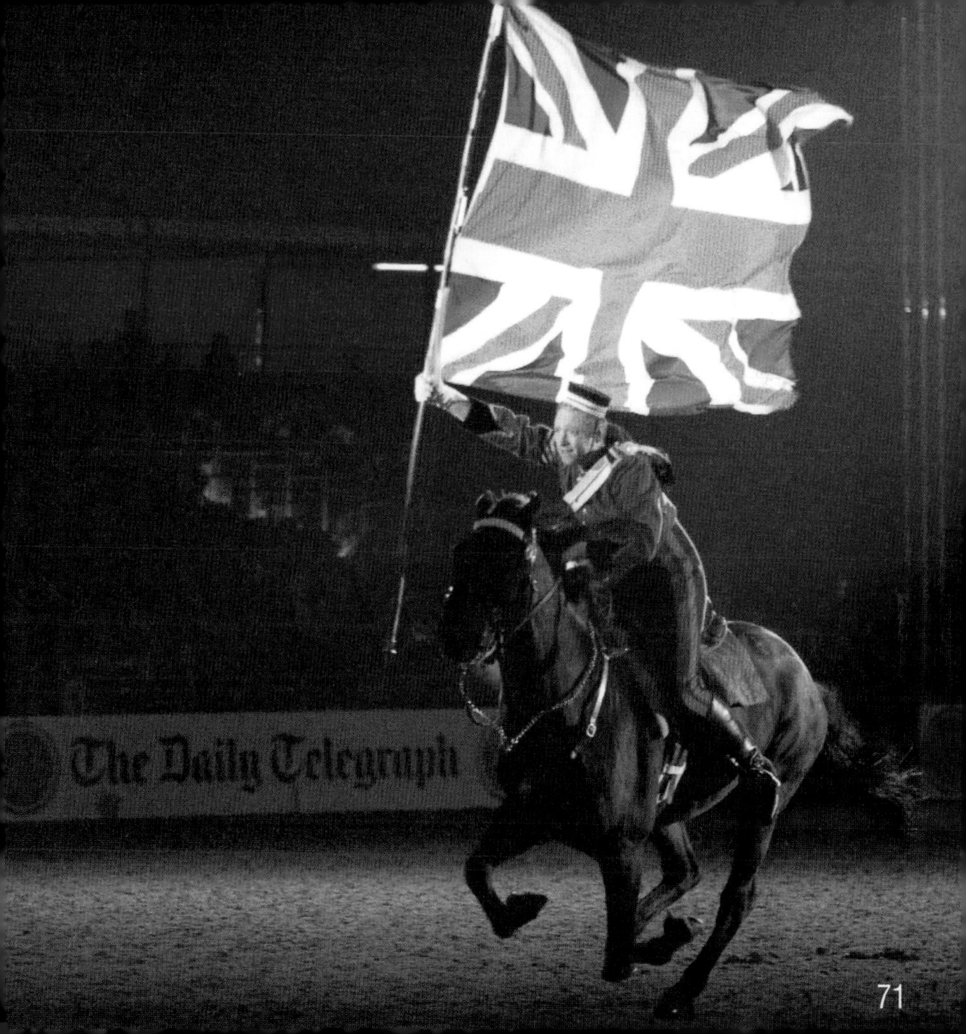
The Daily Telegraph

Cobbled Streets — straight ahead and left of Queen Victoria's Statue when leaving the Castle

The streets in this part of town date from 17th century. The buildings from the south side of Castle Hill to Queen Charlotte Street all have extensive vaults or cellars that extend under the streets.

Windsor has the UK's shortest street, Queen Charlotte Street at just less than 16m (51 feet 10 inches) to the left of the Market Cross House.

The cobbles in Windsor were originally made of wood, some of which were only removed in the 1940s.

In Church Street you can find the names MICK and MARY spelt out among the cobble-stones by whoever laid the cobbles. You will have to look carefully as they are near the garden at the far end of Church Street.

73

Market Cross House

Built in 1687 the design of the building was too tall for the tiny piece of land and now the house leans dramatically to the left.

One possible reason is that when the foundations were being dug there was an argument over the ownership of the land. Everything stopped and the land was fenced off until the dispute was resolved. During that period the ground dried out. It wasn't until the building was complete that the house began to lean.

Another rumour is that the men constructing the Guildhall extension pushed the newly built Market Cross House away from their building.

The more logical explanation is that the leaning has been caused by the builders using unseasoned timbers during its construction, which have warped over time.

Nell Gwyn

There are many different spellings of Nell Gwyn i.e. Gwyne, Gwynne, however Gwyn is the accepted spelling by her family and biographers.

Nell Gwyn was the long time mistress of King Charles II. Nell actually lived in Burford House given to her by the King which is now part of the Royal Mews. There is no evidence that she actually lived in the house in Church Street (pictured on the next page) however this legend is good marketing for local businesses.

Nell Gwyn was originally an orange seller at Drury Lane Theatre and is the only royal mistress in English history to provoke popular affection.

The Church Street of Nell's time was not a pretty place. It was called Fish Street as fish were prepared and sold there. The Council demanded that this only happen in this street because in those days there were no rubbish collections. Moreover, the next street down, now called Market Street was called Butchers Row with similar mess and smells. Now if you were Charles II, would you want to meet your fancy woman surrounded in fish guts and animal entrails?

"Pray good people be civil, I am the Protestant whore", was Nell Gwyn's cheeky retort to the masses pushing her coach after the crowd mistook her coach for that of the unpopular catholic mistress, Louise de Kérouaille.

King Charles II was popular and was known as the Merry Monarch.

King Charles II was a weak ruler and was known to have 13 mistresses, fathered many illegitimate children but produced no heir to the throne.

One story of how Nell Gwyn's oldest son, also called Charles became the Earl of Burford, was that when he was six years old, the King overheard Nell saying "Come here, you little bastard, and say hello to your father." King Charles was so shocked to hear her calling their illegitimate son a bastard that he immediately made him the Earl of Burford. In 1684 King Charles awarded his son, the Earl of Burford, the title of Duke of St Albans and gave him an allowance of £1,000 a year.

Nell's heirs, the Dukes of St Albans, gave their name to the street behind Church Street. The St Albans family were Windsor's first family until the 3rd Duke got into financial difficulties and sold Burford House to King George III for £4,000 in 1777.

Royal Mews

The Royal Mews on St Alban's Street was designed by famous architect Wyattville and can stable 110 horses.

The Mews were finished in September 1842 and cost Queen Victoria £70,510.

Horses used to pull the Royal carriages during Royal Ascot and State Visits are stabled here.

Windsor Greys are the horses, which by tradition always draw the carriage in which The Queen travels.

Shakespeare

William Shakespeare has recently been rumoured to have written his play 'The Merry Wives of Windsor' in a house in Church Street. There is no historical evidence to support this claim!

THE WORLD'S MY OYSTER..

If Shakespeare wrote the play anywhere in Windsor it would have been in the Garter Inn, now the Harte & Garter. In the 16th century there were in fact 2 inns, side by side, the Garter and the White Hart. Shakespeare makes the Garter Inn one of the settings for the play, with the host of the Garter Inn one of his characters. On the inside staircase of the hotel there is a Victorian stained glass window with pictures of Falstaff and other characters from the Merry Wives.

Falstaff, one of his principal characters in the play, ends up being thrown in a muddy ditch close to the Thames in Datchet Mead. Shakespeare must have known that the ditch carried away all of the town's rubbish.

The saying 'The World's My Oyster' is first found in a speech by Falstaff in The Merry Wives of Windsor.

SIR JOHN FALSTAFF

The first performance of The Merry Wives of Windsor probably took place in the Vicar's Hall at Windsor Castle in the presence of Queen Elizabeth I who had supposedly commanded Shakespeare to write the play.

Even today you can still see the words The White Harte on the outside of the Hart and Garter Hotel.

King Charles I
There is a copy of King Charles I's death warrant from 1648 on the front of the building at the far end of Church Street. King Charles I was beheaded in London and the pub previously in this building was called The King's Head.

Fire

The archway from the Parish Church housed the town's fire engine in the early 19th century. The keys to the doors of the fire engine archway were kept by two of the Church Wardens and the Sexton, as you can see from the sign above the arch. The fire engine was a huge tank of water with a manual pump that had to be parked near a supply of water. From this, a human chain had to be formed of people passing buckets to each other. You were lucky if there was anything left of your wooden house and possessions after having to find so many people to help put out your fire.

H G Wells

Opposite the cobbled streets by the HSBC Bank in the High Street is a blue plaque that commemorates the fact that H G Wells, the famous author of The Time Machine and The War of the Worlds, worked at 6 High Street as a draper's apprentice in 1880. H G only lasted 2 months as a draper's apprentice before he was sacked! He was 14 at the time and wrote about his experiences in his book entitled Kipps.

Guildhall

Started in 1687 the building was designed by Sir Thomas Fitch, Surveyor to the Cinque Ports, who unfortunately died before the building was completed. The finishing of the building (1689) was overseen by Sir Christopher Wren who was the architect of St Paul's Cathedral in London.

If you look carefully at the top of the columns supporting the first floor, they are a small distance short of touching the ceiling.

Legend will have you believe that this was a deception by a disgruntled Sir Christopher Wren. The story goes that when the building was nearing completion the local councillors expressed their concern that the building would collapse if unsupported and insisted that central columns be added in the interests of safety.

Local historians say there is no evidence of Sir Christopher's deception. This story only came to light after the extension was built in Victorian times. The extension probably made the original foundations sink and resulted in the pillars becoming detached from the ceiling. This version of events is rather more worrying than the legend!

The open area underneath the council chamber has been used as a corn exchange with a meat and poultry market and parliamentary elections on the ground floor. The chambers above are used for social events such as balls and banquets and most recently weddings and civil partnerships.

Windsor's famous Guildhall should really be known as the Town Hall, as it was never the meeting place of the town's guilds. The town's guilds met at the Three Tuns public house next door, which dates from 1518.

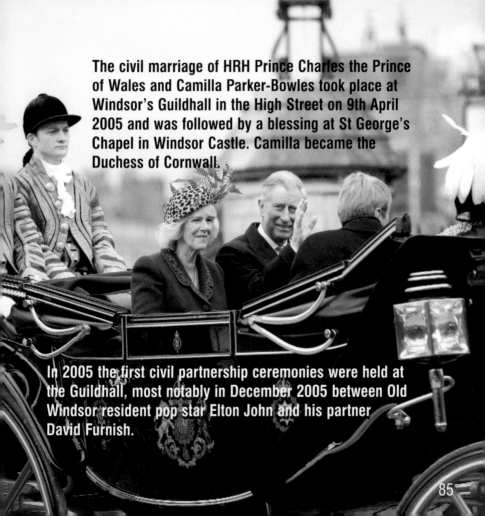

The civil marriage of HRH Prince Charles the Prince of Wales and Camilla Parker-Bowles took place at Windsor's Guildhall in the High Street on 9th April 2005 and was followed by a blessing at St George's Chapel in Windsor Castle. Camilla became the Duchess of Cornwall.

In 2005 the first civil partnership ceremonies were held at the Guildhall, most notably in December 2005 between Old Windsor resident pop star Elton John and his partner David Furnish.

The Parish Church of St John The Baptist

There has been a church on this site since around 1110 when Henry I moved his Court to the Castle from Old Windsor.

By the 18th century the church had increased in size to accommodate 10 side altars. However, in 1818 the high cost of repairs meant that it was more economical to rebuild the church completely, at a cost of £14,000.

In 1822 the new building was completed with cast iron columns and ribs supporting a 25 x 18 metre (84 x 60 feet) roof. The new walls followed the plan of the earlier medieval church and old vaults and memorials were incorporated into the present floor and walls.

A Royal Pew (or Frogmore Pew) is situated on the south side of the Sanctuary. The pew is fronted by a low screen containing panels carved by Grinling Gibbons (1648-1720) each showing a pelican feeding its young. From 1680-1788 the pew formed part of the altar rail in St George's

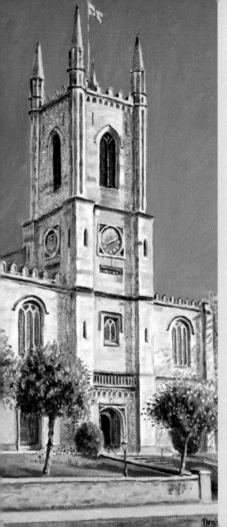

Chapel and George III gave it to the church. You can see Gibbons' peapod signature on the bottom left.

The two thrones within the pew were the gift of Princess Augusta (daughter of George III) who was a regular worshipper here while she lived at Frogmore. The pew was subsequently used for Sunday worship by King George V and Queen Mary when they were living at Frogmore as Prince and Princess of Wales (1901-1910).

The pew was last regularly used by the late Prince George, Duke of Kent, who was killed in an air accident during World War II.

Blue Air Mail Post Box

The original wooden box was erected to commemorate George V's coronation in 1911 and celebrated the UK's first airmail delivery flight which took place in Windsor during the third week in September. Pilot Gustave Hamel flew from Hendon near London to Shaw Farm in the grounds of the Windsor Castle estate.

Test flights went on all week and other pilots were involved before Gustave made the first historic flight. Pilot Charles L A Hubert crash landed soon after take-off breaking both his legs. This was probably the first recorded airmail air crash!

Windsor has the only blue air mail post box in the country! The blue box is situated at the junction of Park Street, St Alban's Street and High Street and dates back to 1934.

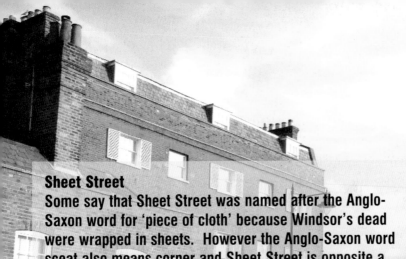

Sheet Street

Some say that Sheet Street was named after the Anglo-Saxon word for 'piece of cloth' because Windsor's dead were wrapped in sheets. However the Anglo-Saxon word sceat also means corner and Sheet Street is opposite a couple of corners! Sheet Street was the location of a pest-house after a plague outbreak in the town in 1603 and subsequently became a poor house, then a prison, then a police station and in 1916 became part of the Victoria Barracks.

The statue on the outside of Royal Albert House in Sheet Street is a copy of the original statue that decorated the outside of the Royal Albert Institute previously on the same site. The original statue is now in the vestibule of the Holy Trinity Church in Trinity Place, just off St Leonards Road.

Long Walk

Charles II created the three-mile-long Long Walk planted with an avenue of elm trees 73m (240 feet) wide from the Castle leading into the Great Park.

The original trees planted by Charles II had to be felled in the 1940s. The avenue is now planted with London Plane and horse chestnut trees.

Frogmore

Frogmore House is located just down the Long Walk from Windsor Castle in the private Castle grounds. The house dates from 1680. Near the house is the Royal Mausoleum, built by Queen Victoria as the resting place for the remains of her husband Prince Albert. Both Prince Albert and Queen Victoria are now interred there. Frogmore House and Gardens are open to the public on a number of days during the summer by kind permission of The Queen.

Prince Albert died in 1861 at the age of 42.

Frogmore derives its name from the frogs which have always lived in this low-lying and marshy area.

The iconic green roof on the Mausoleum is clad with copper from Australia.

Peter Philips (son of Princess Anne) and Autumn Kelly held their wedding reception at Frogmore House after their wedding at St George's Chapel in May 2008.

Royal Farms & Windsor Farm Shop

Royal Farms at Windsor date from the reign of George III who, in 1790, created farms now known as Prince Consort Farm and Shaw Farm situated in the grounds of Windsor Castle.

The Windsor Farm Shop opened in 2001 and was originally the idea of the Duke of Edinburgh to pass on produce, especially meat, from all the Royal Estates.

Beef is supplied from the Royal Sussex Herd at Windsor with Pork from The Norfolk Farm situated in The Windsor Great Park. Hampshire Lambs are reared at Bagshot Park (home of The Earl and Countess of Wessex).

Game is from the Royal shoots in Windsor with some Venison coming down from Balmoral Estate in Scotland.

WINDSOR FARM SHOP

Her Majesty has one of the largest herds of Jersey cattle at Windsor's Home Park which supplies milk, butter and cream to Windsor Castle and the Farm Shop.

Apples and pure apple juices are sold from Royal Fruit Farms in Sandringham.

Situated on the edge of The Home Park, two former Royal potting sheds were converted to house the Windsor Farm Shop.

The shop has a large selection of fresh, local and organic fruit & vegetables.

The Farm Shop cures all its own bacon, cooked hams and makes over 20 different flavours of home made pies.

It only stocks products from small independent companies and considers 'food miles' where possible.

During Royal Ascot, The Queen and her guests leave Windsor Castle in cars and travel down the Long Walk after lunch. The Queen's party then transfers into carriages in Windsor Great Park before arriving at Ascot race course some minutes later.

Snow Hill and The Copper Horse

Famous Victorian novelist Harrison Ainsworth tells us in his book Windsor Castle, that Henry VIII stood on Snow Hill awaiting news of Anne Boleyn's execution which was to be signalled by gunfire from The Round Tower. Nobody knows if this is really true!

Snow Hill is the one of highest points in Windsor Great Park. It was here on 6 June 1977 that The Queen lit a huge bonfire, which was the first of a chain of beacons all over the country to celebrate her Silver Jubilee (25 years). Another bonfire was set alight on 28th July 1981 to commemorate the marriage of Prince Charles and Lady Diana Spencer.

The Copper Horse statue is situated at the end of the Long Walk, at the other end from Windsor Castle and the George IV gateway. The statue of King George III on horseback was erected by his son George IV in 1829 in memory of his father. George IV wanted the statue to be as imposing as that of Peter the Great in St Petersburg so he built it on

There is a story that the sculptor hanged himself after realising that he had completed the statue without putting the rider's feet in stirrups! As the sculptor Sir Richard Westmacott lived to a ripe old age - there is obviously no truth in this rumour!

The statue itself imitates that of Marcus Aurelius on Capitol Hill in Rome who sits without stirrups as they had not been invented at the time of the great Roman Emperors. Stirrups were first used in China in the mid 500s and did not arrive in the west until the late 600s.

The Copper Horse took 5 years to build from 1824 but before the actual statue could be placed on top of the plinth, a leg was damaged in transit when the cart carrying it broke down nearby and a furnace had to be set up on the side of the road to make repairs.

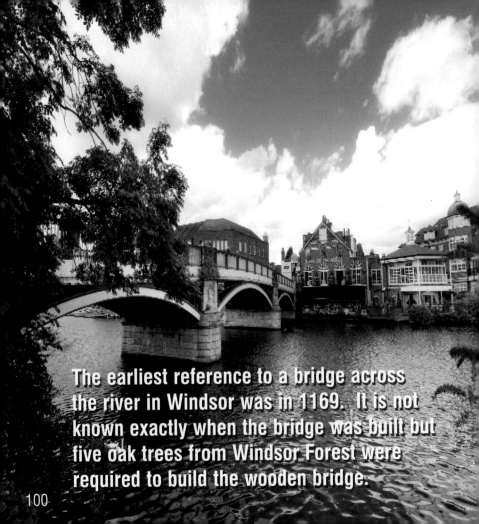

The earliest reference to a bridge across the river in Windsor was in 1169. It is not known exactly when the bridge was built but five oak trees from Windsor Forest were required to build the wooden bridge.

The River Thames

Windsor Bridge to Eton
The present cast iron Windsor Bridge was built in 1822 but there were many different bridges between 1169 and 1822.

Tolls were paid to go over the bridge as well as under the bridge until 1898!

A few days after her coronation at Westminster Abbey in 1953 The Queen and her husband Prince Philip, Duke of Edinburgh entered Windsor via Eton High Street over Windsor Bridge in an open-topped carriage.

Windsor Bridge was deemed unsafe and closed to traffic in 1970. It is now paved and has seats for people to enjoy the river and castle views.

Swans

The annual Swan Upping takes place in July each year and is where the swans on the River Thames are counted and marked by having rings attached to their legs. The ceremony dates back to medieval times when the Crown claimed ownership of all the swans as they were an important food at banquets and feasts. Swans are rarely eaten these days!

The Queen's Swan Uppers, along with the Vintners' and Dyers' livery companies row their six traditional Thames rowing skiffs from Eton Bridge on the morning of the ceremony. The Queen's Swan Marker and the Vintners and Dyers wear traditional scarlet livery with each boat flying appropriate flags and pennants.

It is often said that The Queen owns all the swans but this is not the case. She actually owns about a third of them on the River Thames and shares this with the Vintners' and Dyers' livery companies who were both granted rights of ownership by the Crown in the 15th century.

Flooding

Windsor suffered two severe floods in 1894 and 1947. In 1947 the army were used to reach flooded homes and deliver meals to stranded residents on long poles through their upstairs windows. People living in the areas affected by this flood can sometimes re-animate the smell when redecorating!

When, in 1963 the Thames froze over, champagne was served on the ice opposite the Bells of Ouseley in Old Windsor.

Also in the early part of the century, freezing temperatures and flooding meant that it was possible to skate on the ice covering the Home Park below the Castle.

The man-made Jubilee River was opened in July 2002 by HRH the Duke of York. The river was built to reduce flooding by opening gates at Taplow when the River Thames is high and diverting excess water downstream. It was built specifically to stop Maidenhead, Windsor and Eton flooding.

'I love work, can sit and look at it all day' said Jerome K Jerome in his book entitled '3 Men in a Boat'. The book was meant to be about the History of the River Thames but is more remembered for its wit and commentary.

Just a little way upstream is Brunel's famous Bowstring Bridge, carrying the Great Western Railway on the branch line from Windsor to Slough. The extended series of brick arches pictured here is one of the longest such brick viaducts anywhere in the world and was originally constructed in wood when the railway first arrived in 1849.

The Goswells, Bowling Green and Alexandra Gardens

Today's 'Goswells' consists of bowling and putting greens, tennis courts and a path maze created from an area of Victorian slums. In 1910 The National Trust acquired The Goswells to preserve the views of the castle from the river and Alexandra Gardens.

Alexandra Gardens

A walk around the perimeter of Alexandra Gardens will contribute 1,200 steps towards your recommended 10,000 daily steps.

The Alexandra Gardens were opened by Princess Christian, Queen Victoria's daughter, in July 1902. The Gardens were named in honour of the new Queen Consort, Queen Alexandra wife of Edward VII and Princess Christian's sister-in-law.

Plans to create a riverside garden here date back to Victorian times. However it wasn't until 1895 that the land was finally purchased. In August 1902, to celebrate the Coronation of Edward VII and his Queen, Alexandra, a London Plane tree was planted.

During the summer months The Windsor Wheel is located in the gardens and a land train operates between the adjoining coach park and the Guildhall at the top of the town.

If you have forgotten your watch and the sun is out, you may want to stand on the sun dial near the entrance to the Gardens. To tell the time just stand on today's month in the middle of the sun dial circle and your shadow will be cast on either GMT or British Summer Time.

The Dyson Memorial in the form of a drinking fountain, commemorates Thomas Dyson who became Mayor in 1890. Thomas Dyson actively promoted improvements in the town, including the construction of the riverside promenade.

ETON

Besides Eton College, Eton located just across the river from Windsor, is known mostly for its antique shops, art galleries and curiosity shops.

The Baldwin Institute on the left half way down Eton High Street is where Princesses Eugenie and Beatrice had their first ballet lessons.

The plague reached Eton in September 1606 although the people of Windsor deny it ever reached them.

There is an example of a mid-19th century Victorian post box half way down Eton High Street. It has a vertical slot and the design shows the reason why post boxes were once called 'pillar boxes'.

The restaurant called The Tiger Garden was once called The Cockpit and was a popular location for cock fighting in the 17th and 18th centuries. King Charles II was known to come here to watch the fighting. There are still the remnants of the original cock fighting pits to the rear of the building and a set of original stocks outside.

There is an interesting artwork created near the bridge by the artist Wendy Ramshaw. Brass letters spelling the word ETON are set into the paving stones and there is a 'tower' bollard with a lens for viewing the High Street and the Castle.

Filming in Eton
Chariots of Fire (1981)
A Tale of Two Cities (1980)
The Fourth Protocol (1987)
The Madness of King George (1995)
Wind in the Willows (1996)
Mrs Brown (1997)
Shakespeare in Love (1998)

111

Eton College

Henry VI founded Eton in 1440 as a charity school to provide free education to seventy poor boys who would then go on to King's College, Cambridge, a constituent college of the University of Cambridge, which he founded in 1441. His statue can be found in 'School Yard' in the central quadrangle.

1,300 boys between the ages of 13 - 18 attend Eton, of whom 70 are still King's Scholars.

Eton College has the oldest school room in the world where students have carved their names for generations. Current students are forbidden to do this now!

Princes William and Harry both attended Ludgrove Preparatory School in Wokingham before going to Eton College.

The head teacher (Head Master) at Eton is called the Head Man by the boys. Teachers are known as beaks.

The boys, other than the King's Scholars, are known as Oppidans and are accommodated in 24 houses around the town.

Members of the Eton Society, who act as Prefects, can be identified by their colourful waistcoats. These waistcoats may be passed down from generation to generation.

There is an ornate lamp post in the middle of Eton College called the Burning Bush where boys and masters meet during the mid-morning break.

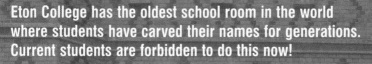

The Fleur de Lys is in the Eton College coat of arms because Henry VI was King of France when he founded the college.

Eton Mess – the delicious summer pudding of strawberries, double cream and meringue mixed together was traditionally served at Eton College's annual founder's day celebration, on the Fourth of June.

The Fourth of June is not celebrated on the 4th June because of terms and summer holidays.

The cannon on display in the Cannon Yard was captured during the Crimean War.

Famous Etonians

- Princes William and Harry
- Earl Charles Spencer, Diana the Princess of Wales's brother
- Tom Parker-Bowles son of the Duchess of Cornwall
- Four times Olympic Gold Medal rower Sir Matthew Pinsent
- Conservative Party Leader David Cameron
- Mayor of London Boris Johnson
- Actors Hugh Laurie and Damien Lewis
- 18 Former British Prime Ministers including Walpole, Pitt The Elder, Gladstone, Harold MacMillan & Alec Douglas Home
- Aldous Huxley - Writer, Brave New World and The Doors of Perception (Rock legends The Doors named themselves after this book)
- George Orwell, whose pen name was Eric Blair, who wrote Animal Farm and 1984
- Poets Percy Bysshe Shelley and Thomas Gray
- Two signatories on the US declaration of independence: Thomas Lynch and Thomas Nelson

Dorney Lake - 2012 Olympics

Dorney Lake is the purpose built rowing lake adjacent to the River Thames, just west of Eton.

The lake is privately owned and financed by Eton College which spent £17 million developing it. Although it is primarily for use by Eton College, the facilities are made available to the rowing community (as well as for canoeing, dragon boat racing and triathlon training).

Dorney Lake will be used in the summer of 2012 as the venue for rowing, canoe and flat water kayaking during the London Olympics. 20,000 temporary seats will be installed for the event.

The lake is 2,000m in length, 13.5m wide, 3.5m deep with 8 lanes of still consistent water conditions – ideal for rowing!

Last time the Olympics were in London was in 1948 and on 30th July Gordon Wigley of Windsor Harriers carried the Olympic flame through Windsor Great Park to Eton bridge on its way to Wembley.

From time to time Formula One driver, Jenson Button can be seen racing at Dorney Lake. OK, not with his Formula 1 car, but in one of the many triathlons that take place there throughout the year.

Princess Anne competed for Great Britain in the three day equestrian event at the Montreal Olympics in 1976. 'The horse is about the only person who does not know you are Royal' she is reported to have said.

THE HORSE IS ABOUT THE ONLY PERSON WHO DOES NOT KNOW YOU ARE ROYAL

Windsor Great Park

The Windsor Estate is 15,000 acres and includes Ascot Race Course and three golf courses. Windsor Great Park covers 4,500 acres.

Windsor Great Park is the only Royal Park managed by the Crown Estate whose responsibility it is to maintain the Park's unique character.

HRH Prince Philip, Duke of Edinburgh is the Ranger of Windsor Great Park as was Prince Albert, Queen Victoria's husband.

The speed limit in the Great Park is 38 miles per hour which is 50 kilometres per hour.

The old gnarled deciduous trees of Windsor Great Park are now the last known dead wood habitats of 5 species of saproxylic beetles otherwise known as click beetles.

Herne's Oak
Herne the Hunter was a mythical Royal game keeper. Apparently he used to wear stag antlers on his head so that he could get closer to the deer to hunt them.

Herne the Hunter was a favourite of Richard II and hung himself in the Park. Legend has it that his ghost can still be seen riding through the park on a black stallion at the head of a pack of black hounds, complete with the stag antlers attached to his head!

In fact the original Herne's Oak was felled in error in the 1790s and another tree was christened Herne's Oak in order to hide the mistake.

In the 1860s the tree rumoured to be the actual tree (or was it the second tree?) from which Herne hanged himself was felled and Queen Victoria burnt the oak logs in an attempt to kill the ghost.
Whichever tree it was, old Herne is still around and has been spotted many times since!

Deer have been kept in the Great Park for centuries. However the deer were removed to Balmoral, The Queen's estate in Scotland, during the Second World War in 1940 when large areas of land in the park were turned over to food production.

In 1979, at the suggestion of The Duke of Edinburgh, 1,000 acres of the park were enclosed and the deer reintroduced. The deer you see today are from the original stock sent to Balmoral in 1940.

George IV used to keep a giraffe and menagerie of other animals in Windsor Great Park. Unfortunately the giraffe died!

On September 30th 1940 Oberleutenant Karl Fischer of Jagdgeschwader 27 was flying his Messerschmitt 109 on a bomber escort mission to London. After the plane was hit he landed the plane on its roof in Windsor Great Park. The plane was subsequently righted and put on display at the top of the Long Walk. Locals paid sixpence a time to view the plane and the money raised went to the local Hurricane Fighter Fund. The young Princesses Elizabeth and Margaret were taken to see it.

Coincidentally, Sir Sydney Camm the designer of the Second World War Battle of Britain fighter, the Hawker Hurricane, was born in Windsor and was educated at the Royal Free School.

Sydney Camm was one of Britain's most distinquished aircraft designers and responsible for the design of over 40 planes. He helped develop vertical take-off and landing (VTOL) which is still a feature in some of today's planes.

To commemorate his aeronautical achievements a full sized replica Hawker Hurricane is planned for Alexandra Gardens in 2010.

The lakes, woodland and historical landscapes of The Savill Garden and The Savill Building, The Valley Gardens and Virginia Water are collectively known as The Royal Landscape.

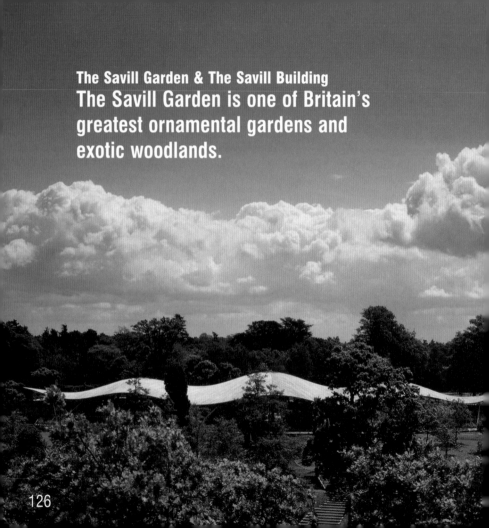

The Savill Garden & The Savill Building

The Savill Garden is one of Britain's greatest ornamental gardens and exotic woodlands.

Developed under the patronage of Kings and Queens, The Savill Garden was created in the 1930s by Sir Eric Savill. It began as a woodland garden, with native oak, beech and sweet chestnut trees, but has since evolved by incorporating many new plants over the years.

The Savill Garden has many interlocking gardens such as Spring Wood, The Summer Wood, The Hidden Gardens, The Summer Gardens, The Glades, Autumn Wood, The Azalea Walks and The New Zealand Garden. Each is a garden within a garden.

In June 2006 the Savill Building opened. Designed by Glenn Howells Architects the building uses a gridshell construction, a landmark feat of contemporary engineering, inspired by the strength and beauty of a seashell.

Twelve miles of sustainable larch and oak timber from the Crown Estate forests were used in the 90 metre-long and 25m wide building. The impressive single space has an apparently self-supporting gridshell roof.

The building has won many awards for using wood from sustainable resources, and its design and construction.

Polo at Smiths Lawn

Smiths Lawn area is now the largest area devoted to polo in Europe, with 12 grounds.

Polo is played here most weekends during the summer. Polo is divided into time periods known as 'chukkas'. Between chukkas the riders may take a few moments to leave the field and change ponies.

In the 1950s the spectators were first invited to walk onto the pitch in between chukkas to tread the divots – saving the groundsmen many hours of work trying to restore the surface after the game.

The Queen and members of the Royal Family are often to be seen watching the Polo from the Pavilion. You can tell if The Queen is watching as a Royal Standard can be seen flying above.

Both Prince Charles and The Duke of Edinburgh were skilled players; today Princes William and Harry are also accomplished players.

The Cartier International Polo held at Smiths Lawn each July is a 'must' in the social calendar.

The Duke of Edinburgh is said to have undertaken flying lessons from Smiths Lawn.

Smiths Lawn was once a heath and used as an airfield in the Second World War.

131

The name 'Smiths Lawn Plantation' was first recorded around 1748, a lawn in this case being a glade or pasture in a deer park.

Troops camped out on Smiths Lawn in August 1915. It seems likely that the camp was for training purposes before the troops set off for the front in northern France.

During the First World War, in 1916, the Canadian Forestry Corps, sent to support the war effort made their headquarters at Smiths Lawn. For a short time after the war, Smiths Lawn was known as The Canadian Camp. The Canadians were amazed at the size of some of the oaks in the Great Park, one having a circumference of 38 feet, which was probably around 1,000 years old.

In World War II, Smiths Lawn was used as an aerodrome. The airfield would have permitted a quick escape route in the event of a German invasion for the monarch, King George VI, Queen Elizabeth and their two princesses, Elizabeth and Margaret.

Totem Pole

Visitors are surprised to discover a 100 foot high totem pole in the Great Park near Virginia Water. The totem pole was erected in 1958 and was a gift to HM The Queen from the native peoples of the northern part of Vancouver Island. The totem pole celebrates the centenary of British Columbia being proclaimed a Crown Colony by Queen Victoria on 19th November 1858. It was carved from a 600-year-old Western Red Cedar tree by Indian Chief Mungo Martin one of the finest craftsmen of Totem Poles.

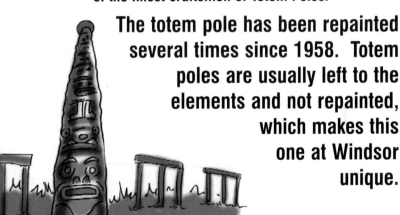

The totem pole has been repainted several times since 1958. Totem poles are usually left to the elements and not repainted, which makes this one at Windsor unique.

133

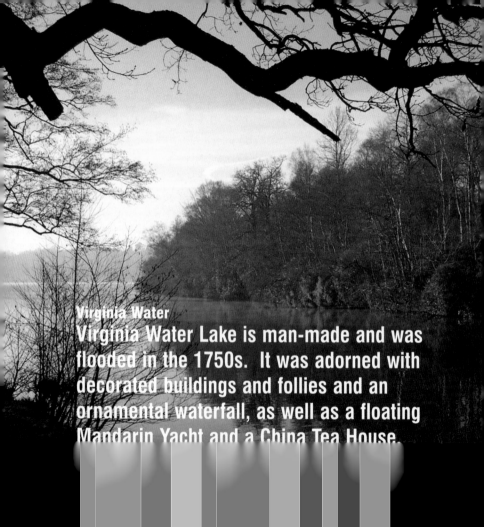

Virginia Water

Virginia Water Lake is man-made and was flooded in the 1750s. It was adorned with decorated buildings and follies and an ornamental waterfall, as well as a floating Mandarin Yacht and a China Tea House.

At the end of the lake are 'imported' ruins which come from Leptis Magna on the coast of the Mediterranean near Tripoli.

In 1816 the local Governor in Tripoli was persuaded that the Prince Regent (later George IV) should be able to help himself to the ruins. The local people were outraged and obstructed efforts to remove the columns and stones, so much so, that some of the ruins were even left on the beach in Leptis Magna!

After 10 years of transport difficulties and a stay at the British Museum, the ruins finally started to arrive in Windsor in August 1826. It took 12 journeys and three months on gun carriages to complete the transportation of the 37 columns, 10 capitals, 25 pedestals and various other slabs.

After 150 years the ruins needed to be repaired and rebuilt and in May 2009 a restoration was completed. The ruins were restored to a ruinous state!

135

Located on the northern shores of Virginia Water are the 250 acres of The Valley Gardens. This flowering forest has grassy meadows and many exotic shrubs and has been continuously planted since the middle of the 18th century.

Visitors can enjoy native trees, such as sweet chestnut and scots pine flourish alongside flowering cherries, azaleas, magnolias (including The National Collection of Magnolias), exotic oaks, sweet gums, tupelos, Asiatic rowans and maples.

The Japanese Kurume Azaleas in the Valley Gardens' Punch Bowl were first collected by the English plant hunter Ernest Henry Wilson in 1918 and were planted in The Valley Gardens between 1948 and 1950.

Cranbourne Tower

Cranbourne Tower was originally part of Cranbourne Lodge built in the reign of Charles II and was visited by Samuel Pepys in 1665. The Tower is all that remains now. The area is one of the highest points in the Windsor Great Park and water from the Romney Lock Pumping Station was stored in this area to supply surrounding areas using a gravity feed system.

Great Park Village

The Great Park Village is worth a visit but is accessible only on foot, bike or bus. The village was built in the centre of the Great Park in the 1930s, to house Royal estate workers.

There is a small Post Office and general store where ice cream and refreshments can be bought.

In the first BBC documentary about the Royal Family. The Queen was shown to buy Prince Charles and Princess Anne an ice cream from the village shop.

Queen Anne's Ride

Queen Anne's Ride, runs south-west towards Ascot and dates from 1708. The Ride is a grand avenue similar to The Long Walk and is also three miles in length.

Queen Anne is rumoured to have driven her specially designed hunting chariot, fast and furiously!

Fort Belvedere

Fort Belvedere was built around 1750 on the Windsor Estate but was not converted into a residence until 1911. The property was later given to Prince Edward, then the Prince of Wales by his father, King George V. The Fort became the Prince's main residence even after he became King Edward VIII in 1936. Edward continued to use the Fort for entertaining. It was here that he conducted much of his romance with the twice divorced Mrs Wallis Simpson. Fort Belvedere is now a private residence.

Edward VIII ruled for 325 days and his abdication proclamation was signed at Fort Belvedere and his abdication speech was broadcast from Windsor.

His coronation date had already been set and souvenirs still exist to commemorate the coronation of the King who was never crowned.

Due to Edward VIII's abdication the throne went to his brother (Queen Elizabeth II's father). As everything had already been arranged for the coronation, King George VI was crowned that day instead.

The House of Windsor

House of Windsor

Sovereigns normally take the name of their House from their father. For this reason, Queen Victoria's eldest son Edward VII belonged to the House of Saxe-Coburg-Gotha (the family name of his father Prince Albert).

Edward VII's son George V became the second king of that dynasty when he succeeded the throne in 1910.

On 17th July 1917 George V adopted the surname Windsor after the Castle and town.

Kings and Queens sign themselves by their first names only, a tradition which continues today.

144

The Queen

Princess Elizabeth and the Duke of Edinburgh were in Kenya when she was pronounced Queen upon the death of her father, King George VI. The proclamation was made in Windsor at the statue of Queen Victoria just outside The Castle.

In 1953 the Queen insisted that her coronation be televised and thousands of people bought televisions especially to watch.

Queen Elizabeth II is the fifth British sovereign to reign for 50 years or more. She is now the oldest ever British monarch! Queen Victoria died in 1901, aged 81.

There are no obligatory codes of behaviour when meeting The Queen or a member of the Royal Family, but many people wish to observe tradition. For men this is a neck bow (from the head only) whilst women do a small curtsy - other people prefer simply to shake hands.

On presentation or meeting The Queen the correct formal address is 'Your Majesty' and subsequently 'Ma'am' (pronounced Mam to rhyme with jam).

When The Queen is in residence at the Castle, signs hang around the Windsor estate so that the staff know that the 'boss' is around.

The Queen rarely drives on public roads but often drives herself to engagements around Windsor Great Park.

Engagements include driving to watch members of her family play polo at Smiths Lawn or to Chapel in the grounds of Royal Lodge on a Sunday. Sometimes her husband Prince Philip is her passenger!

The Queen does not carry money.

One of the few times The Queen does carry money is when she attends Church. On this occasion she will take a freshly ironed £10 note for the collection tray. One of The Queen's footmen does the honours with the iron.

The Queen loves corgis and received her first corgi named Susan from her parents on her 18th birthday. All her subsequent corgis have been related to Susan and The Queen can often be seen walking her dogs in the Castle grounds.

The Queen sometimes carries dog biscuits, mints and a camera in her handbag.

The Queen does not need a passport nor does she have number plates on her official car.

'A glass of wine with lunch? Is that wise? You know you have to reign all afternoon!' Her Majesty The Queen Mother was overheard saying to her daughter The Queen.

The Crown Estate
The Crown Estate is valued at over £6 billion and owns commercial properties, agricultural land, forests and residential property throughout England, Scotland and Wales. The Crown Estate is one of the largest rural landowners in the UK (146,000 hectares or 60,000 acres).

The Crown Estate owns 55% of the UK's foreshore, tidal river-beds and almost all the seabed for 12 nautical miles.

149

Windsor through the Ages

The first Royal Wedding took place in Windsor in 1121 between Henry I and his second wife Adelizia of Louvain, the 'Fair Maid of Brabant.'

Windsor Castle was under siege in 1193 for two months by barons opposing Prince John's coup attempt. Years later John became King and on 15th June 1215 King John made his way from Windsor Castle to Runnymede, just the other side of Old Windsor. Here he was forced to put his seal on the Magna Carta by the barons who believed he was abusing his Royal powers. After sealing the Magna Carta he was besieged again at Windsor for three months.

The Magna Carta was the very first charter to quantify certain civil liberties.

The four original copies of the Magna Carta have been given World Heritage Status by the United Nations and admitted to the Memory of the World programme by UNESCO.

Windsor's earliest known Charter was granted on 28th May 1277. The Charter meant that Windsor was no longer administered by the Constable and Governor of the Castle, but became a free Borough, responsible for managing its own affairs.

In the mid 14th century plague struck the country at a time when Edward III was busy rebuilding much of the castle at Windsor.

In 1362 writs were issued to find an additional 302 masons and stone diggers to replace those who had died from the Black Death.

During his lifetime John Schorn gained a reputation as a healer of ailments, including malaria, rheumatism and eye afflictions. After his death in 1314, scores of pilgrims visited his burial place in North Marston, Buckinghamshire, in order to display piety, perform penance and in the hope of gaining a cure or witnessing a miracle.

So substantial was the fame and profitability of Schorn's pilgrimage centre at North Marston that the Dean of Windsor, Richard Beauchamp, decided to purchase Schorn's bones and relocate them to St George's Chapel. Beauchamp secured a licence for the transport of the bones in 1478 from Pope Sixtus.

By 1528 there were 20 alehouses in Windsor – that's rather a lot for a town with a population of barely 1,000.

Three of the five Windsor Martyrs, Henry Filmer, Anthony Pierson and Robert Testwood were burnt at the stake on 28th July 1543. The fourth, Robert Bennett, escaped execution as he was suffering from the plague (he subsequently recovered!) and the fifth person accused, John Marbeck, was the organist of St George's Chapel. He was deemed to be too useful musically to be executed.

In 1563 Queen Elizabeth I fled from London because the bubonic plague was rife around the city. She travelled to Windsor to escape. According to legend she set up a gallows at Windsor to hang anyone else following her example.

Plague is rumoured to have reached Windsor in September 1606, but the townsfolk were quick to deny it. There is however, a record of the plague in Eton.

Charles I was held prisoner at Windsor during the 4 weeks before his trial in London in January 1649. His body was brought back to Windsor on 7th February and two days later laid to rest in the vault in St George's Chapel beside Henry VIII and his third Queen, Jane Seymour.

Queen Anne and her husband Prince George of Denmark had 18 children together (7 daughters, 5 sons and 6 still births).

William, Duke of Gloucester was their only child to survive but only until the age of 11. Because there were now no descendants, an Act of Settlement was necessary assuring the succession of the Throne to a Protestant heir. The two subsequent Hanoverian kings weren't very popular and neither particularly liked Windsor and during their reigns (1714 - 1760) the castle was neglected and fell into disrepair.

Queen Anne established the first racing on the heath at Ascot in 1711.

During the early 1800s there were several 'black ditches' carrying waste from the higher lying parts of Windsor to the lower lying Goswells and Clewer where the poor lived. The ditches flowed into the Thames above the bridge.

By 1801 Windsor's population had increased to 3,361 of which 239 lived in the Castle.

Queen Victoria and Prince Albert spent their honeymoon at Windsor after their wedding on 10th February 1840.

Queen Victoria took her first railway journey from London Paddington to Windsor at a speed of 44 miles per hour. Prince Albert thought this was far too fast!

Prince Albert, Victoria's beloved husband, popularised Christmas tree decorating following the German custom of his homeland.

In 1841 he set up a Christmas tree at Windsor Castle. The Illustrated London News published the famous picture of the 'Christmas Tree at Windsor Castle' in 1848. The tradition of decorating a tree at Christmas has stayed with us ever since.

However, as early as 1800 Queen Charlotte (wife of George III) had made a candle lit tree the spotlight of her Christmas celebrations.

The marathon of 1908 started at Windsor Castle and finished 26 miles 385 yards (42.195 km) away at the Great White City Stadium at Shepherd's Bush. Originally 26 miles exactly in length the extra yards were added so that the spectators (including Queen Alexandra) could have the best view of the final yards of the race. The finish line was in front of the Royal Box.

Windsor experienced an earthquake in the middle of a June night in 1931. Luckily there was no loss of property.

John Corby manufactured valet stands in Windsor from 1930 onwards. Later a pressing area was added and the first Corby trouser press was launched. These became electrically heated during the 1960s and can be seen in homes and hotels all over the world.

During the Second World War, high explosive bombs and V1 and V2 missiles fell on the town. A crater, caused by a bomb dropped on 24th October 1940 at 5.30am, can still be seen in Clarence Crescent Gardens near the junction of Clarence Crescent and Clarence Road.

Princesses Elizabeth and Margaret lived at Windsor during the Second World War - their parents King George VI and Queen Elizabeth used to visit each weekend.

A bomb killed local resident Bill Wing who was riding his bicycle in Vansittart Road close to Maidenhead Road when the bomb fell.

HRH The Duke of Edinburgh was made an honorary Member of Windsor & Eton Rotary Club in 1958.

The Sixth and Seventh National Jazz and Blues Festivals were held August 1966 & 1967 at Royal Windsor Racecourse. 40,000 people attended over 3 days but outgrew the race course and the Festival found a permanent home in Reading. The Reading Festival is still going strong today!

The 1967 Festival's main musical claim to fame was the first ever appearance of Peter Green's Fleetwood Mac and there were also appearances by The Small Faces, The Move, Tomorrow, Marmalade, The Nice (who replaced Pink Floyd, who had to cancel due to the musical incapacity of Syd Barrett), Paul Jones, The Crazy World Of Arthur Brown, Ten Years After, Amen Corner, Cream, Jeff Beck, Donovan and Denny Laine.

Windsor's population had trebled during the 20th century and many small houses close to the town centre were replaced by a massive block of flats called Ward Royal 1969. Ward Royal is now considered by many to be the least attractive building in Windsor. Not all history was lost when they built the estate however, as a little way along the pathway by the boundary wall on the southern side of Ward Royal, you can see the remains of the end walls of air raid shelters.

In 1970 the bridge joining Windsor and Eton was closed to vehicles and has remained a pedestrian bridge ever since.

Doris Mellor became a national heroine and was awarded an MBE in 1977 following her battle to preserve Windsor's Bachelors Acre. After lengthy research she registered the space in the centre of the town as a Town Green. The local council and planners had wanted to build a multi-storey car park and she opposed this. Doris and the council went from court to court and eventually she took them all the way to the Court of Appeal, where on 20th May 1975 Lord Denning supported her Town Green registration. The car park was never built and residents have enjoyed the space ever since.

In the 1970s a Chapter of Hells Angels bought a house in Maidenhead Road. After one of their members died under suspicious circumstances his lying 'in state' at the house lasted for two weeks before 400 Hells Angels rode through the town on the day of the funeral.

For a time the elephants from Windsor Safari Park (now Legoland) were kept at quarters within Billy Smart's Circus in Winkfield about a mile away. At the end of the day the elephants were led home. Passing motorists had to avoid the huge piles of dung in the road en route between Windsor and Ascot.

Legoland opened in 1996 on the former site of Windsor Safari Park.

The Royal Windsor Shopping Experience is built on Station Approach which was once George Street. This area of the town was known as a den of iniquity because of the number of bawdy houses, cheap lodging and brothels.

Prince William celebrated his 21st Birthday at Windsor Castle in 2003 with a huge party.

Prince Harry is a serving British Army officer in the Blues and Royals, a regiment of the Household Cavalry. Prince Harry was decorated with the Operational Service Medal for Afghanistan by his aunt, the Princess Royal, at the Combermere Barracks in Windsor in May 2008.

Windsor is the 19th most expensive place to live in England.

The Princess Royal is pictured here after presenting shamrocks to the Irish Guards on St Patricks Day on 17th March 2009.

Windsor Environs

Lower Town Centre
Prince Consort Cottages were built by Prince Albert. People who lived here had to get certificates to prove to Queen Victoria their honest, sober and industrious habits.

Joseph Chariott built Almshouses in Windsor. He kept his money in pickle jars in his basement and after his death at the age of 91, relatives loaded his jars into a cart to take the money to the bank. Rumour has it that the bottom fell out of the cart, the jars smashed and the money had to be collected from all over the road.

Clewer

Clewer or Clifware is thought to refer to the people who lived below the 30m (100 feet) white chalk cliff outcrop overlooking the River Thames on which William the Conqueror build his wooden fort.

The Saxon font in St Andrew's Church in Clewer is decorated with peas and beans which were widely grown in the area.

Peascod Street - the town's main shopping street is a derivation of pea pod.

The convent in Hatch Lane was original built in the early 19th century for the nuns from the Anglican Community of St John Baptist. They were a teaching and nursing order and worked in the UK, India, the West Indies and America.

The convent was initially known as the House of Mercy because if offered a refuge to women who had fallen on hard times, the homeless, the abused and those who had found their way into prostitution.

These women, after training, were offered employment outside the Convent but those who chose to stay entered a special order known as the Magdalens. Some of them are buried in St Andrew's churchyard. The nuns moved to Begbroke near Oxford in 1998 and the convent buildings were sold for redevelopment.

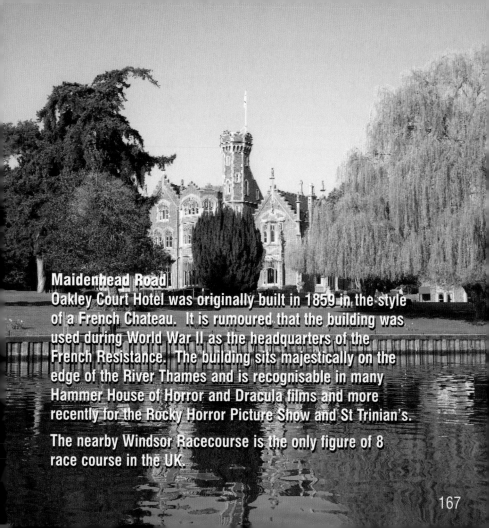

Maidenhead Road

Oakley Court Hotel was originally built in 1859 in the style of a French Chateau. It is rumoured that the building was used during World War II as the headquarters of the French Resistance. The building sits majestically on the edge of the River Thames and is recognisable in many Hammer House of Horror and Dracula films and more recently for the Rocky Horror Picture Show and St Trinian's.

The nearby Windsor Racecourse is the only figure of 8 race course in the UK.

BRAY FILM STUDiOS

Bray Studios was the home of the Hammer House of Horror films from 1951 to 1967.

The model and miniature filming for the sci-fi classic Alien was done at Bray Studios in 1978.

In 1984 the video 'Do They Know It's Christmas' was shot at Bray Studios.

Today, rock bands book their pre-tour rehearsals here as entire stages with lighting, sound and projection rigs can be constructed, prior to taking the show on the road.

Old Windsor
Old Windsor was the original location of the town of Windsor.

The remains of a Saxon palace, excavated in the 1950s, still lie under a field near the church.

There is a branch of Battersea Dogs Home here finding new homes for rescued dogs and cats from the area.

Runnymede
The Magna Carta was sealed at Runnymede and to commemorate this the American Law Society built a memorial.

In addition, there is also a memorial to John F Kennedy just off the meadow and on top of the hill there is the Air Force Memorial built by the Commonwealth War Graves Commission to remember the 20,000 men and women who were lost without trace during World War II.

Bray

Diana, Princess of Wales frequently took her brother Charles Spencer for lunch at the Hinds Head in Bray when he was at school at Eton.

Heston Blumenthal - famous restaurateur, owner and chef at the Fat Duck in Bray also now owns the Hinds Head pub in Bray. The Fat Duck is one of only a handful of Michelin 3 Star restaurants in the country. In 2005 Heston Blumenthal was voted the Best Chef in the World by his peers and top food critics.

The Waterside Inn is owned by Michel Roux and family and also has 3 Michelin Stars.

Bray is the only village in the world with two 3 Michelin starred restaurants.

Billy Connolly and his wife Pamela Stephenson used to live in Bray in a house called Chateau Bateau.

Slough

Founded in 1920, Slough Trading Estate is the largest single privately owned industrial estate in Europe. The Trading Estate covers 486 acres (1.97 km^2) of commercial property and has 500 businesses and a working population of 20,000 people.

Mars Bars were first manufactured by American Forrest Mars in Slough in 1932.

The famous slogan "A Mars a day helps you work, rest and play" was written by William Dagnall as a competition tie breaker in 1966.

Sir John Betjeman the UK's Poet Laureate (1972 -1984), wrote a poem about Slough and its Trading Estate. 'Come friendly bombs and fall on Slough! It isn't fit for humans now ......' He later regretted writing the poem and often said that he had not meant it.

The world famous Pinewood Studios is situated just outside Slough, home to the James Bond 007 stage.

The Bourne Ultimatum, Brideshead Revisited and The Dark Knight are just a few of many other blockbusters filmed at Pinewood.

Ascot
The Royal Ascot race meeting takes place during June each year, although Ascot is an all year round racing venue.

The annual race meetings now attract 550,000 people over the year with 300,000 coming to Royal Ascot alone.

During Royal Ascot, bets are placed each day on the colour of The Queen's hat.

The Queen is an owner and breeder of her own racehorses. Jockeys riding Her Majesty's horses wear The Queen's racing colours - purple body with gold braid, scarlet sleeves and black velvet cap with gold fringe. The Royal Silks have remained the same since 1877.

The Queen has satellite TV installed at the Castle so she can watch the racing!

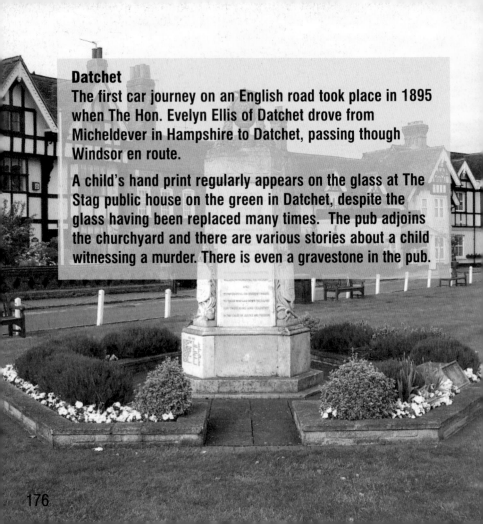

Datchet

The first car journey on an English road took place in 1895 when The Hon. Evelyn Ellis of Datchet drove from Micheldever in Hampshire to Datchet, passing though Windsor en route.

A child's hand print regularly appears on the glass at The Stag public house on the green in Datchet, despite the glass having been replaced many times. The pub adjoins the churchyard and there are various stories about a child witnessing a murder. There is even a gravestone in the pub.

Windsor in Film and on TV

On The Beat, Norman Wisdom 1962

Carry On Again Doctor, 1958 & Carry On Cabbie 1963 -
Sid James, Kenneth Williams, Charles Hawtree, Jim Dale,
Hattie Jacques, Joan Sims, Barbara Windsor,
Peter Butterworth, Patsy Rowlands

The 70s TV Detective Series called The Professionals
starring Martin Shaw, Lewis Collins and Gordon Jackson.
Windsor Arts Centre was used as the Police HQ building.

King Ralph (1991)
Tomb Raider (2001)
Thunderbirds (2003)
As You Like It (2005)
Crooked House (2008)
Harry Potter (2003/2004/2010)
Ridley Scott's Nottingham (2010)

177

Windsor in Print
In 1992 Bill Bryson wrote with great amusement about Daniel's Department Store, in his book 'Notes from a Small Island.' Luckily Daniel's has had several revamps since then and remains a favourite store with locals and Daniel's toy department is known for miles around!

Famous Windsor Residents Past & Present

Historical
William Shakespeare and Nell Gwyn.

Sir Christopher Wren lived here as a child.

Sir Daniel Gooch, who made the first steamship capable of laying the cable across the Atlantic, lived at Clewer Park in Windsor. He was made a baronet and was the first engineer to be knighted.

Geoffrey Chaucer author of The Canterbury Tales came here in 1357 as a page in the household of the Countess of Ulster.

Dr Samuel Johnson visited his friend Topham Beauclerk (one of the St Albans family) and is recorded to have lain down on one of the table-top tombstones in the parish churchyard.

Fanny Burney, pioneer women novelist, who wrote Evelina, served Queen Charlotte at Windsor Castle for five years from 1785.

William Herschel, Astronomer to George III, lived for a time in Old Windsor and then Slough. He often came to court to show the heavens through his telescopes. George III once encouraged the Archbishop of Canterbury to walk through the tube of the great twenty foot telescope Herschel was building saying 'Come, my lord Bishop, I will show you the way to Heaven'.

Mary Robinson, nicknamed Perdita, is buried in Old Windsor churchyard. She was spotted by the 17-year-old Prince of Wales (later George IV) when appearing in Shakespeare's The Winter's Tale. The Prince fell madly in love with her and showered her with letters and gifts and promised eternal love if she would leave the stage. She did but the affair lasted less than six months. After struggling with her health she was left a cripple at the age of 26 but went on to embark on a successful career as a poet and a novelist.

The famous hymn 'The Church's One Foundation' - was written in Windsor in 1866 by Parish Church curate, Rev. J S Stone (1862 - 1870), who lived in the curious gatehouse in Bachelor's Acre.

Margaret Oliphant - 19th century novelist and historical writer lived at Clarence Crescent. Today the house is called Oliphant House.

James Bedborough - Davina McCall's great, great, great, great grandfather - a stone mason from Windsor Castle and latter day property developer built large areas of Windsor. He was Mayor of Windsor twice!

Alfred Young Nutt 1867. Architect, surveyor and designer of the present Royal Vault and much of St George's Chapel.

Novelist Thomas Hardy came to Windsor as a young architect and oversaw the building of All Saints Church in Frances Road. Architectural plans with notes in his handwriting are on display on the walls of the church.

Sport
Sir Nick Faldo - famous golfer and former Ryder Cup Captain lives in Old Windsor.

Explorers
Sir Ranulph Fiennes was born in Windsor in March 1944.

Political
Joseph P Kennedy, father of John F Kennedy lived in the white Georgian mansion in the grounds of Legoland when he was US Ambassador to Britain.

Admiral Alan West, The Lord West of Spithead GCB, DSC Parliamentary Under-Secretary for Security and Counter-terrorism and former First Sea Lord and Chief of the Naval Staff

> "I found your book fascinating having lived in Windsor during a very formative period of my life (1955-1961) attending Dedworth Green Junior School and Windsor Grammar School. Although I was only young when I lived there, Windsor helped mould me into the person I am now. My parents later moved back to the Thames Valley and so I visited often and indeed still do."

Film

James Bond/007 actor Daniel Craig has lived in Windsor on and off whilst filming at Pinewood Studios.

Actor Michael Caine lived at the Old Mill House at the end of Mill Lane, Windsor during the 1960/70s.

Voluptuous screen siren of the 60s and 70s Diana Dors died in Windsor on 4th May 1984. She lived in Ascot.

Music

James Blunt was barracked in Windsor when he was serving as a Captain in the Lifeguards Household Cavalry Regiment.

Elton John and David Furnish own a home in Old Windsor where they hold lavish parties every year.

Natalie Imbruglia - Australian pop and Neighbours star lives on an island in the Thames.

Jimmy Page of Led Zeppelin lived in Windsor until 2004 after buying the Mill House from Michael Caine.

Rod Stewart, Ringo Starr and John Lennon all lived on the Ascot edge of Windsor Great Park in the 1970s. Ringo still lives there.

TV/Radio

Anna Friel - Actress

"I've lived in Windsor for nearly 10 years now and love it. The majesty and beauty of the town and Castle are breathtaking and every day I'm here I enjoy stepping out of my back door and walking in the beautiful Long Walk and Windsor Great Park. In Windsor my family and I are part of the community, my daughter goes to school down the road, I enjoy a drink at the local, cycling to the shops and spending time with my friends and neighbours. My partner, actor David Thewlis and I, are proud to have become patrons of The Fire Station, Windsor's very own arts centre."

Kris Marshall - Actor

"As a Windsor resident of over 10 years I consider myself a true local despite it not being the place of my birth. It never fails to enrapt me; especially after months away filming in foreign climes. That first view of the town, its river and castle (often from the air on the final approach into Heathrow) always fills me with a sense that, finally I am home. I hope to savour that unique feeling for many years to come."

Rob Brydon had David Walliams as an usher at his wedding at the Parish Church in 2006.

Sue Holderness who plays Boycie's long suffering wife Marlene in 'Only Fools and Horses' has lived here for many years.

Freddie Starr once lived in a house called My Way in the famous St Leonards Hill area.

Terry Wogan's daughter and son-in-law run a restaurant in Oakley Green.

Rolf Harris, artist, muscian and TV presenter lives in Bray. The BBC commissioned Rolf to paint a portrait of the Queen to commemorate her 80th birthday.

Sir Michael Parkinson - TV chat show host used to live in Trinity Place in Windsor and now lives and plays cricket in Bray.

Windsor is the home of 1981's Mastermind & International Mastermind Champion Lesley Grout who answered questions on St George's Chapel.

Three women from Windsor have appeared on the BBC2 series Dragons' Den. Charlotte Evans & Carolyn Jarvis (Buggyboot) and the author of this book, Caroline Wagstaff with her BackBliss back lotion applicator and back scratcher. (Well, I had to get a mention in somewhere! www.backbliss.com)

Food
Celebrity chef Anthony Worrall-Thompson owns a restaurant and delicatessen shop here.

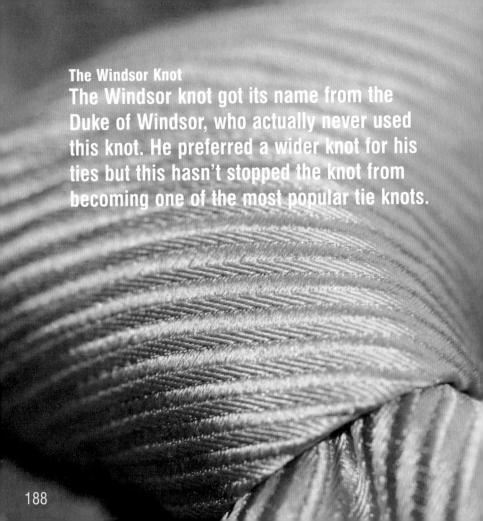

The Windsor Knot
The Windsor knot got its name from the Duke of Windsor, who actually never used this knot. He preferred a wider knot for his ties but this hasn't stopped the knot from becoming one of the most popular tie knots.

All Things Windsor

Brown Windsor Soup
Brown Windsor soup is a typical hearty thick British soup that was popular during the Victorian and Edwardian eras. The soup generally contains lamb or beef steak, parsnips, carrots, leeks, bouquet garni and Madeira wine.

Brown Windsor soup was one of the starter dishes on the menu at the fictional Fawlty Towers!

Windsor Ontario, Canada
Windsor is the southernmost city in Canada and lies in Southern Ontario with views of the US city of Detroit's Skyline. The city was originally called Sandwich but was later renamed Windsor after Windsor in Berkshire.

Red Windsor Apple
Red Windsor is an aromatic Cox like apple but sweeter and more disease resistant than The Cox. Ironically the apple originates from Herefordshire (100 miles from Windsor).

Windsor Red Cheese
Berkshire's only native cheese is a cheddar impregnated with veins of elderberry wine – delicious!

Windsor Chair
A Windsor chair is built with a wooden seat into which are fixed the backrest and undercarriage. Typically, the backrest and sometimes the arm pieces are formed from steam bent pieces of wood. Windsor chairs were developed in the late 17th century in High Wycombe (about 15 miles from Windsor). They were loaded onto boats in Windsor to go to London and the boxes were marked 'Windsor'.

Barbara Windsor
Well known for her appearances in the series of Carry On films and as the matriarchal Peggy Mitchel in EastEnders.

Frank Windsor
Frank played Detective Sergeant John Watt in the 1960s police series Z Cars and played the same character in the spin-off series Softly, Softly from 1966 to 1976.

Windsor Davies
Most remembered for his ear drum shattering military scream and catchphrase of "Shut Up!", Windsor Davis played Battery Sergeant Major Williams in the sitcom 'It Ain't Half Hot Mum' (1974-81). Windsor also had a number one UK hit with a version of "Whispering Grass" which he recorded with his co-star, Don Estelle.

The Duke and Duchess of Windsor
Edward VIII's and his new bride Mrs Wallis Simpson became the Duke and Duchess of Windsor.

Useful Websites

www.windsor.gov.uk – Tourist Information including travel, accommodation and general information

www.windlesora.org.uk – Windsor Local History Group was formed in 1976 to research the history of the town. They have published several books and their regular Windlesora journal which features the people and places of Windsor.

www.windsormuseumappeal.org.uk – Friends of the Windsor & Royal Borough Museum

www.rbwm.gov.uk/web/museum_index.htm – Windsor & Roayl Borough Museum.

www.theroyalwindsorwebsite.com – Windsor past and present historical reference web site

www.royalcollection.org.uk – The Official web site for Royal Palaces and Residences – Click Windsor Castle

www.stgeorges-windsor.org – The College of St George including St George's Chapel

www.theroyallandscape.co.uk – The Savill Gardens, Savill Building, The Valley Gardens & Virginia Water

www.thecrownestate.co.uk – The Crown Estate

www.royal.gov.uk – **The official site of The British Monarchy**
www.berkshirehistory.com – **Royal Berkshire history website**
www.sirsydneycamm.org – **Memorial and bursary appeal**
www.visitthames.co.uk – **The River Thames from source to sea**
www.rwhs.co.uk – **The Royal Windsor Horse Show**
www.windsortattoo.com – **Windsor Castle Royal Tattoo held on the evenings of the Royal Windsor Horse Show**
www.windsorfarmshop.co.uk – **Local produce - some from Royal Estates**

www.britishlegion.org.uk – **The Royal British Legion Caring and campaigning for the serving and ex-Service community**
www.helpforheroes.org.uk – **Support for Armed Forces Wounded**
www.army.mod.uk – **The British Army**
www.raf.mod.uk – **The Royal Air Force**
www.royalnavy.mod.uk – **The Royal Navy**

www.theroyalboroughimagebank.co.uk - **for all images of Windsor**

This book is dedicated to my Mum and Dad, Rosemary and Michael Wagstaff, who met in Windsor and lived here for many years. Thank you for your love and support. Dad, I wish you could see this!

My special thanks to the passionate Windsorians I have met along the way. Your help, advice and knowledge have made this book an honour and pleasure to create. Your enthusiasm for all things Windsor was infectious.

I've written the sort of book I would like to read, full of affectionate, quirky and unusual facts. Hopefully you will agree!

Caroline

Words of ART

My personal thanks to:-

Members of the Windsor Local History Group: President: John Hancock, Chair: Hester Davenport, Secretary: Susan Ashley, Editor: Pamela Marson, Treasurer: Barbara Mitch, and members Roger Cullingham, Margaret Gilson, Beryl Hedges, Elias Kupfermann, Brigitte Mitchell, Norman Oxley, Patrick Rooney, Joyce Sampson, Sonia Sayed, Geoffrey Try, and Kathleen Whelan Julia White, Visitor Manager, Royal Borough of Windsor & Maidenhead Sue Watt, Centre Manager, Windsor Royal Shopping, Jamie Gorst Capital Hosting Capt Simon Nichols MBE, Irish Guards Blue Badge Guides Hilary Thompson, Hugh Burn, Leslie Grout, Hans Kjaersgaard, Jacqui Kjaersgaard Charlotte Manley LVO OBE, College of St George, Windsor Castle Christine Taylor, Visitor Manager, Windsor Castle Nick Day, Operations Manager and Gino Caiafa, The Crown Estate Chris Murray, General Manager, Royal Farms, Windsor Farm Shop Penny Hatfield, Archivist, Eton College Sammy Morgan, Artique Publishing, Dr David Murray Bruce, Chairman, The Windsor & Eton Society.

Finally huge a thank you to my friends Anne Wingrove, Bronwen Eustace, David Clyne and Mandy Hall for your patience and unfailing good humour, no matter what.

NOW ITS YOUR TURN

- Tell me what you thought about the book
- If you know a fascinating fact that should be included in the next edition
- If you have a wonderful photograph that I could use next time
- If you've spotted something that needs correcting
- If your town or city needs a book like this

Email: caroline@words-of-art.com

Call: +44 (0) 1753 861091

To order more copies of this book

www.words-of-art.com/windsor